The *Life*

The *Life*

Is it Mystical or Real & Painful or Magical?

Magical Pathways to Magical Life.

S.P. CHOCKALINGAM

PARTRIDGE

A Penguin Random House Company

To order additional copies of this book, contact
Partridge India
000 800 10062 62
www.partridgepublishing.com/india
orders.india@partridgepublishing.com

CONTENTS

Dedication

Dedicated to Ammani, my mother, Ponniah, my father, Sundaram, my maternal uncle, who showed the Way to think truthfully, to talk truthfully and do truthfully and laid the Path to travel and for what my family and I are today.

The author had a unique privilege of meeting His Holiness Dalai Lama in Jakarta in 1983. He shook hands with him and held his hands for sometime and conversed with him. This meeting had a transforming and everlasting influence on the author.

Introduction

There was a saying. Madras was a village. The metropolitan city is now called Chennai, in India. It has changed its face in many ways. But the sea near the Marina Beach remains as beautiful as ever. The second longest beach in the world only next to the beach in Rio de Janeiro in Brazil continues to be the pride of Chennai.

It was early morning in December. The cool breeze from the sea was soothing to the body and the mind. The whispering of the tides of the sea was providing music to the steps of the walkers who were taking regular walk in the morning on the pathway near the beach. After taking my regular walk, I sat on a bench under a tree. An old gentleman was also sitting on the bench engrossed in looking at the beauty of the blue sea with its rising white waves. I had seen him in the beach quite often. But I never had the courage to talk to him.

He was tall and serene with a smiling face and always dressed in spotless white dress. He must have crossed seventy five. His smile was infectious and his laughter was instantaneous. He used to talk with a voice of music, filled with love and compassion. He was unique and stood out as a giant in the midst of the walkers' crowd when he walked along with them. He was greeted by everyone with reverence. For every one who used to take a walk on the beach, he appeared to be a yogi. Although I used to see him very often on my regular walk and used to hear him whenever he talked to others, I never spoke to him. That day, I gathered courage and decided to talk to him.

"Good Morning, Sir. I am Lingam. I come to the beach for a regular morning walk. I have been seeing you regularly on the beach and wanting to talk to you. May I know your good name, Sir?"

"Name, I have no name. I am nobody. It was Tao Te Ching who wrote that 'the name that can be named is not the eternal name.' This fits with humans so well. This is what ultimately happens."

"Is it not strange? Without name how can one identify the other?

"Identity; is it for useful purpose or for divisive purpose? Originally it was intended only for useful purpose. But over time identity is misused, abused, exploited, and used for purely *personal gain* resulting in humans' problems and misery. For identification, divisions are made; boundaries are laid out; labels and titles are attached. It begins with the divisions of nations, states, cities, towns, villages, hamlets, color, race, creed, gender and religion. Then education, caste, community, muscle power, money power, political power, position and status, titles in work place, and political affiliations etc. are kept on added. The pyramidal system of life provides fertile field to keep on planting divisions and boundaries for selfish purposes. These divisions and boundaries are widening and growing endlessly causing conflicts, misery and suffering."

"Is it not the way the human life is organized? What can you and I do about it?"

"You and I can do a lot. A simple good thought, good idea, good word, good deed, and correct action at correct time can bring change. A good thought can produce waves of goodness all round. A good idea can revolutionize the whole world. A good word can become code. A good sentence can become a quotable quote. A good deed can become a model of action. Some of them can become eternal. Human history is full of such events of change which helped humans to evolve themselves.

On the other hand, empires were established, palaces were built, and statues of kings, queens, and rulers were erected. At what cost? These were done at the cost of human lives and peoples' money, only to perpetuate a few names and their titles. This happens even in the 21st. Century, for the leaders, rulers, actors, and even for tom, dick and harry. But one after the other all of them had fallen and are falling at the footsteps of time when time marches on its own.

But, the words of Aristotle, Socrates, Plato, Vyasa, Valmeehi, Krishna, Buddha, Jesus, Mohammed, Milton, Shakespeare, Confucius, Tao, many other sages and saints of India, and poets of Tamil Sangam Age of South India, although originally passed on by word of mouth for generations and also written in leather, silk, palm leaves, pop up even today and remain alive in spite of the ravages of time.

If everyone feels as you feel then there is no salvation. Everything starts from *the individual*. "It is the action, not the fruit of the action that is important. You have to do the right thing. It may not be in your power, may not be in your time, that there will be any fruit. But that does not mean you stop doing the right thing. You may never know what results from your action. But if you do nothing, there will be no result." This is what Mahatma Gandhi said.

If one starts changing, the other will follow and the virus will catch up with everyone.

Richard Brodie's 'Virus of the Mind' is quite revealing. According to my understanding of this virus, imitating, copying, following will go hand in hand from one mind to another's mind and spreads like virus.

One can say that if it is for good, the virus catches with many. The same is with the bad but the velocity of speed of this kind of virus is much more than the other. This keeps happening. But if you do not want to do anything good, then nothing happens and the opposite takes over everything.

Once a rich and powerful person started to feel at the height of his achievements that 'something was missing' in his life. This feeling of 'missing' grew day by day and made his life miserable. He wanted to find out the answer. He therefore went to meet a Zen Master in a monastery up the hill and waited for the call after he sent in his identity card with gifts. His card with his name boldly printed described a number of his qualifications and his positions in social, political and economic activities.

He waited for the whole day but he was not called in by the Master whereas all others who were less important without even having any identity card and looked very ordinary were called in and met by the Master. He was annoyed and went home dejected. He went back three times to the monastery and presented his different cards and different gifts but nothing worked. Fourth day he went and waited without sending in any card and gifts.

He was called in by the Master. When he explained his problem to the Master, the Master said that 'he was living all along with illusion and on the fourth day he himself realized that without any identity he was recognized as a human. This self-realization is the first step towards the path of enduring happiness whether one was rich or powerful or poor."

"Thanks. May I proceed? Are you from Chennai or north?"

"No. I belong to everywhere. I am a tiniest molecule Part of the Universe and the Universe as a Whole is part of me. In other words, I am in the Universe and the Universe is in me."

"What are you doing, Sir? Business, or Industry, or . . . ?"

"I am doing nothing. The works for the existential livelihood or money or power or name or popularity or control when done only to satisfy one's personal gain purely for selfish purposes and to satisfy one's ego do not have any real, intrinsic, enduring value. Doing nothing helps one to realize that who is he or she and ultimately leads one to freedom and peace.

However, I have been spending a lot of my time in the mandapams (open halls with10, or 100, or 1000 stone pillars) of the temples, steps of the mosques, corridors of the churches, benches in the parks, shops and malls, sitting, watching and talking to people from all walks of life. In such occasions many people whom I met used to share their problems and I used to share my knowledge with them as solutions for many years.

Now I am spending my time in Marina Beach with beach walkers. Some of those who had earlier shared their problems and shared my thoughts have now become beach walkers.

They now share their experiences after they experimented with what I have discussed with them earlier and the changes which had taken place in their lives. I still share with them whatever I could now offer to them. This is the way my business of the day goes on."

"Are you living alone or with your family?"

"I never live alone. I live with everyone; live for everyone. I belong to the entire world. The entire world belongs to me; not for ownership and exploitation; but for creation, sustaining, protection, giving and receiving and serving. Living only for oneself and one's family is as meaningless as a small dust perching on a chain of diamonds (life) which is a wonderful gift given to everyone by unknown source."

"In that case who takes care of you?"

"I take care of myself. My mother used to tell me that the 'One who planted the tree will always provide water to it.'" In other words everyone will always get some help or other when in distress from some unknown source and at uncommon hours. This is the way the life goes on and on."

"You mean to say that life comes and goes on its own way."

"Yes, of course. Not only it comes and goes on its own way but on its own time. It is true of everything."

"Then what about human efforts and works."

"All will have to happen on account of evolution. Even after all that efforts and works, what happens? Changes keep happening and uncertainty remains. But everything happens as per its own nature and on its own terms. Every turn of life is still unpredictable?"

"You mean that life itself is uncertain and unpredictable?" "Uncertainty is only certain in life."

"Is it therefore mystical?"

"Life is more mystical than any other mysteries in the world. It is the mother of all mysteries. However much, the philosophers and scientists try their best to unfold the mysteries of life from time to time it reveals piece by piece but hides most part of it still. At the same time life is more real and painful for many than any one can predict or imagine."

"Why humans with all their ingenuity could not change life into a happy existence?"

"Every human wants to be happy. But each one looks outside than inside, to get happiness ignoring the reality. When reality asserts itself, the suffering, pain and sickness manifest to the bewilderment of humans. This happens in every generation; also generation after generation. But if one follows and walks the magical pathways then one can certainly mitigate the suffering, pain, and sickness. "

"Do Nature, Time, and Health play important role in life?"

"Yes. Nature provides every other ingredient to humans to have life, live, and co-create in the process of evolution. It also strikes sometimes very severely in unexpected ways and plays havoc of destruction of lives and humans' creations on earth. But if one respects nature and provides healthy participation and lives close to it without exploitation then nature will allow the humans to play the role of co-partner in evolution without much of suffering, pain and sickness. Time is one of the self inflicted wounds by humans on themselves. Health of course has become the core aspect of human existence which will have to be understood, nurtured, protected, and taken care of till the end."

"Why then people talk about Karma, Destiny, Fate and Luck?"

"These are the words for excuses and convenient escape routes to explain away the unexpected and uncertain happenings in life such as serious sickness, pain, and sufferings and sometimes about unexpected happenings of good things in life."

"What about Religion and Spirituality?"

"Ritualistic, dogmatic, and materialistic religions are failing to help humans to save their lives from sickness, suffering and pain; also failing to lift them up from emptiness to fullness. Genuine belief and faith are being overshadowed by noisy, unnecessary, and unproductive rituals. Truthful worship is being sidelined by extravagant spending of money on rituals, festivals, and anything related to religion. When money dominates every aspect of religion then the divinity of religion vanishes from the threshold of religion. Faith is slowly shifting towards spirituality."

"Do you mean Happiness is elusive?"

"Happiness is one thing which is always misunderstood for instantaneous pleasure. Looking out for conditions to bring happiness has become the habit of humans. Looking outside rather than inside is like chasing the mirage."

"Are there ways to acquire enduring happiness and make life magical?"

"Correct Choices and Balance, Yoga and Meditation, determining and following the Purpose and Meaning of Life and Magical Pathways if one chooses to take and proceeds to walk through will help to make the life magical."

"Thanks. However I would like to know what you mean by Magical Pathways."

"These are the pathways which I have been advocating whoever comes to me for free advice to meet the different kinds of challenges which life throws out on each one's life's journey at different points of time. Many had come back and told me that these pathways had magically changed their lives. Then I decided to call them as Magical Pathways. I will tell you some of such real life stories with their pseudo names to protect their privacy when we go along the path."

When the old man was talking to me and before I recover from his unusual and radical views on life, a young man of around forty whom I used to see sitting and talking to the old man came and sat near him.

The young man looked like a modern executive who was in hurry to climb the success ladder and typical of a modern rat race runner fitted with multi-colored tight half trouser, tight tea shirt, gadgets like a mobile phone, ear phone around his neck, ears and a hat on his head and multi-colored shoes. He had come for a walk fully equipped!

I was taken by surprise by the answers of the old man. However I wanted to pursue my conversation.

"Sir, I know that both of you sit here and discuss for a long time. Sometimes, I was listening to your discussions. I was benefited. I strongly feel that I should make them available to others as well. I want your permission to record your conversations. May I have your permission?"

"Why do you want permission for recording?"

"Sir, one day I would like to publish it for the benefit of the present generation."

"Permission nowadays is not given; it is taken. Anyway, as I said earlier, I would prefer to be anonymous. Same is with my young friend. Also, there is no need to use any pseudo names."

"If it is so, how do I call these discussions?"

"You may say, "The Life". You may also include saying

"Is It Mystical or Real and Painful or Magical?"

"Thank You Sir."

I took leave of him. The rest is the dialogue on THE LIFE . . . .

CHAPTER 1

The Life

Is It Mystical, or Real and Painful, or Magical?

Life is an opportunity; benefit from it.
Life is beauty; admire it.
Life is bliss; taste it.
Life is a dream; realize it.

Mother Teresa

The sun was rising from the other end of the sea. The Marina Beach was quiet, cool and pleasant in the early hours of the day. The sun's golden rays reflected over the sea waters and made a golden path to the shores of the sea. The tides were gently jumping in the golden rays of the sun on the path in their joyous moment of the beginning of the day.

The golden path was shining and inviting. It looked as if nature, with the sun, sea and sand, exhibited a coordinated event of joy and dance. Those who had the eyes and the mind to see and enjoy would not have missed nature's bountiful beauty.

This is what John Ruskin meant when he said, that "Nature is painting for us day after day, pictures of infinite beauty, if only we have eyes to see them."

The golden path over the sea looked as if it was specially laid out for those who have reached a higher level of consciousness to walk on it and reach the eternal light on the other side of the sea of life.

A gentleman was sitting as usual under the tree on a bench on the shore of the beach and looking at the golden path with a joyous smile on his face. It looked as if he will one day walk on the golden path and cross

1

over to the eternal light. He was about seventy five. He looked contented, serene and happier. A young man of about forty came and sat near him. He looked a man in hurry and lost in his thoughts. The young one wished the old one and started his dialogue.

"Good morning; Sir, May I sit down here? I was looking forward to talking to you. But your stature and the way the walkers on Marina Beach greet and respect you put me off. Today I gathered some courage and decided to talk to you. Will you have time?"

"Young man, why do you think so? You are welcome. I am a human being as you are. We are interconnected whether we see or talk to each other. It will be my pleasure to talk to you. Time is always my servant and not my master. You can meet me and talk to me whenever you come to the beach."

"Life seems to be mysterious. Is it not more difficult and complicated nowadays?"

"One has everything today. The human mind and intellect have conquered the hitherto unknown areas of science, technology, medicine, biology, psychology and even the mystery of nature's creation. Man is close to finding the mind of God. He is trying to create humans in the labs. Man is reserving space on the moon to build houses to live. Man is going to Mars and other planets to find water, other resources and their inhabitants. As far as the material and creature comforts are concerned, one has unimaginable advancements in life. One has a tiny mobile in hand that can bring the whole world instantly to see, hear, talk and write to anyone across the world. Still, how can one say that life has become more difficult and complicated now?

Anthony de mello once wrote that, "Life is a mystery, which means, your thinking mind cannot make sense out of it. For that you have to wake up and then you will suddenly realize that reality is not problematic, you are the problem."

"Life is really simple,
but we insist on making it complicated."
Confucius

Imagine the plight of Stone Age's humans and their lives. Humans have traveled a long path to reach the present Knowledge Age. If the *mind*, which has achieved all these advancements, remains unchanged as far as the *personal life* is concerned, without a shift in the level *of consciousness, then* life becomes difficult and complicated. Ludwig Wittgenstein said that, "We feel that even when all possible scientific questions have been answered, the problems of life remain completely untouched."

It was Mahatma Gandhi who said that "As human beings, our greatness lies not so much in being able to remake the world . . . . as is being able to remake ourselves." Positive mind vibrates and attracts positive reactions from others and life itself. Similarly negative mind will attract negativity all round. This is what Ken Keyes Junior wrote, "A loving person lives in a loving world. A hostile person lives in a hostile world. Every one you meet is your mirror." Here, a story comes to my mind:

'Once a villager who lived in the mountains was going to a village in the valley to find out whether he can shift from mountain to valley. On the way, he met a monk who was sitting under a tree. He asked the monk whether the village was a good place to live and whether the people were friendly and helpful. The monk asked, 'what was his experience in his village in the mountains?' The villager replied that life was very difficult and complicated as the people were very unfriendly and selfish. The monk told that the villager might find the same way of life in the village in the valley as well. The villager felt unhappy and left.

After some time, another villager from the mountains came on his way to a village in the valley and met the monk. He too wanted to know about the life in the village in the valley and the people who lived there.

The monk asked how life in his village in the mountains was and how he felt about the people there. The villager replied that life was happier and the people were good and friendly. The monk told the villager that he would find the same way of life in the village in the valley. The villager thanked the monk and proceeded happily to his destination.'

This old story reflects the way life presents itself to one as per the attitudes of his mind. Attitude is the core aspect of human existence. Attitude is everything in life. According to attitudes we live our lives either happily or unhappily. Attitudes are important in deciding our choices we make, the friendships we cultivate, the habits we develop, and finally the way we decide to live our lives.

One day Arnold met me when I was sitting in the corridor of an old church. He was 45, masters from an elite school, married with working wife and one baby boy, CEO of an I.T. company with a big home and fat income. He narrated his story and said that no one liked him in home, in office and also outside. Whatever he was trying to do there were hurdles and frustration was mounting. Having everything, he felt that his unhappiness was growing day by day. He was in search of happiness. He went on holidays, visited health retreats for solving his problems, and tried to get relaxation in going to gyms, consulted psychiatrists but nothing seemed to have helped him. He was looking lost and felt something was seriously, may be his karma, working against him.

After I listened to him, I told Arnold that looking inward may help to identify problems. Other humans are the mirrors of your own image and inner self. If you feel hostile to others, others will feel the same way with you. On the other hand if you feel happy with everyone then every other human will similarly feel happy with you. What one feel, think, talk of others and do to others will come back to the same human in the same measure or sometimes in more severe quantum. Yoga and Meditation will help one to look inward, relax body and mind. Good intentions, faith, trust, empathy, prayers, humility, gratitude, compassion, appreciation and love are the pathways which will take him to his destination of happiness. Arnold took my views seriously and promised to follow those pathways with commitment and took leave of me.

Now, coming back to your question that life is also mysterious, Albert Einstein wrote "the most beautiful emotion we can experience is the mystical. It is the power of all true art and science".

No one knows where from and what purpose one has taken the present avatar. No one knows why one is born as a male and the other a female. No one knows who he/she is and why is he/she here on this planet. Khalil Gibran himself felt the same way and he wrote, that "Only once I have been made mute. It was when a man asked me, who are you?"

Also, no one knows where one goes after death. At what time life begins its journey as human in the womb is still unknown. What will happen the next moment is not known. Why the past has happened in the way it has happened is not known. Why the present is happening as it is now happening is also not known.

Also, for some, life is magical. Those who identify and follow magical pathways in their day to day life get what they want in life. They feel that life is magical. However, for many, life is real and painful. Whether the life is magical or real and painful, the fact remains that it is shrouded in mystery. But why should one worry about the mystery? Mystery by itself is beautiful. Life is also as beautiful as the mystery. It is the greatest gift one can have in the world. One, by living the life, will have to find answers to these questions. Mystery will unfold itself in the course of one's life provided one leads a meaningful and purposeful life."

"What originally appeared as a simple mystery now it appears to be a complicated mystery? One is born as a baby and dies when becomes old. In between, one struggles through a life of ups and downs, pleasure and pain, health and sickness, prosperity and poverty, happiness and sorrow. These appear to be real and impact everyone without exception in life. That is why I told that life is very difficult and complicated now. You seem to be more philosophical than practical."

"Philosophy is derived from the existential experiences of human life. Some humans at one time or other feel that life is mystical. Many who experience pain and sufferings feel that life is real and painful. But those who follow magical pathways and achieve what they want in life realize that the life is magical. These are the experiential and practical truths of life. They are neither philosophical nor imaginary.

Those who feel life is mystical can enjoy the mystical part of it which is not under the control of any human. But wherever possible they can change it to reality by changing their attitudes. Similarly those who feel life is real and painful can also make life magical by taking and following the magical pathways. Finally everyone can change the life into a magical life. It is in their hands. It is achievable. One can make it happen. When it happens, then life becomes a magical life.

But what you told is the duality of life, which happens in one's life. Krishna, Buddha, Jesus, Mohammed, Ramakrishna, Vivekananda, Confucius, Tao and many others have laid the path to travel and overcome the duality. If one finds his own way to enter the magical paths to travel, then one can dissolve the duality and discover that life is not difficult and complicated.

Nature itself works on the basis of duality: Sun and moon, hot and cold, day and night, light and shadow, water and fire, earth and sky, peaks and valleys and so on. Sometimes they become the metaphors of the human life and also interconnected. These are the facts of life.

> "Both light and shadow are the dance of love".
> "Through your loving existence and non-existence merge.
> All opposites unite.
> All that is profane becomes sacred again."
> **Rumi**

"Sorry. I am still not able to get the correct understanding of what you say. May I request you to take me slowly on your less traveled path, which I have not yet attempted to tread?"

"Yes. I will do. First, what is life? Oxford Dictionary says that life is 'a state of being alive as human being'. This means, besides the body, which is a visible form of a treasure, invisible treasures are hidden inside the body.

They make the body to function and being alive. It is called spirit, prana (breath), life force, vital energy or life itself. In addition, there is mind. The seat of the spirit, or the self, or the consciousness, or the soul within the body is still shrouded in mystery. The present Neurologists say that the seat of the mind is in the brain. The powers of the spirit and the mind are infinite. What we know till now is only a fraction of what is hidden inside.

The sages and the seers found some of them using their mind's eye.

The present day scientists are trying very hard to identify and locate them. Still their identification and locations are elusive.

According to Neurologists the seat of the mind is in the brain. Some say that each limb of the body has its own mind. However in practice all these three, the body, the spirit and the mind will have to work harmoniously for the normal functioning of the human being. In other words, one will have to realize the importance of the body, the mind, and the spirit and nurture, and ensure their proper growth on a well-meaning path. "Human life is nothing but an as semblance of vital energy. When it comes together, we come to life, when it scatters, we die". This is the saying of third century Chinese philosopher, Chuang—Tzu.

The fundamental law of nature is to create, grow, sustain, dissolve and recreate. The growth takes place in the body, the mind, and the spirit over time after birth. The question is how the growth takes place is important. One will have to love, nourish and sustain them constantly till the end. These three should never be abused and misused. There are three fundamental conscious awareness and practices one should constantly observe in one's life with regard to the mind, the body, and the spirit. If this is done, life will become worth living with health, wealth, peace, joy and happiness."

"You mean to say that one has control over the growth of the body, the spirit and the mind?"

"Yes; of course. If you sow good seeds, you will reap good harvest. If today is made good, tomorrow will certainly be good. When foundation is good, then the structure built over it will be strong. The first is regarding the mind. One will have to practice right thinking, right words, right feelings, right emotions, right choices and right deeds from childhood to the end. Napoleon Hill wrote that "Whatever the mind can conceive and believe, it can achieve."

> **"The cultivation of the mind is a kind of food supplied for the soul of the man."**
> **Marcus Tullius Cicero**

It is absolutely important to keep the mind engaged and challenged in learning so that one can ensure its proper growth. The mind can grow to the extent of maximizing its power which is infinite.

"I understand. Perhaps these old ideas may not fit in the present rapidly changing modern ways of life. However much one tries, it is very hard when it comes to practice. I keep trying but I am unable to practice. Perhaps the materialistic and consumerist ways of life and the competitive rat race do not permit me to practice. One who practices may lose out in competition and therefore may lose the opportunities, progress, wealth and life itself. Please put me on the right path."

"It is not true. The Earth, water, air, and sky are as old as the Universe. The nature keeps on renewing them every time and they become fresh and new for the renewal of life in the old planet of ours to sustain the life system of everything in the Universe including the lives of the humans. Similarly, the old teachings and sayings of Buddha and other saints and seers of ancient times are as fresh and new as ever. Humans will have to rediscover, reinvent, renew, and reorient them in the present modern, hasty, and fast changing world in order to make humans' life magical.

The exponential advancement in science and technology, other disciplines, and various other areas of human life have impacted the day to day life of the humans.

In addition, the globalization, commercialization, and consumerism have also brought about series of changes in the life styles of the humans.

These changes have thrown up new and powerful challenges to the humans. These challenges stare at the faces of the humans in everyday life. They appear from the areas of nature, time, health, choices, religion, spirituality, purpose and meaning of life, and happiness. To meet these challenges many of the old teachings and sayings have now become more relevant and essential natural therapy for healthy living. As long as the body, the mind, and the spirit remain intact these teachings and sayings whether old or reinvented will help the humans to renew, heal, and meet the new challenges with success for healthy, happy, and peaceful life.

As I told earlier, it is the mind and not the present way of life that causes the problems. You know we are made up of both physical and non-physical matter. The physical body, although it appears solid, is a bundle of energy in vibration. The spirit and the mind, although they appear invisible, are very powerful elements. In totality, humans have electromagnetic power, which vibrates into the atmosphere. Similarly, the vibrations of the universe impact humans.

Both are therefore interconnected as well as humans with one another and also with every other thing in the world. These are the present scientific findings.

> **"A human being is part of a whole, called by us 'universe', a part limited to time and space."**
>
> **Albert Einstein**

The Sufi philosopher and poet Rumi has also echoed the same view saying that "The whole universe exists inside you. Ask all from yourself." In Vedic Scriptures it is said that "As is the microcosm, so is the macrocosm. As is the atom, so is the Universe. As is the human body, so is the cosmic body. As is the human mind, so is the cosmic mind."

If one understands the significance of these sayings, one can direct the attention to the mind. If the mind is trained and disciplined only to right thinking, right words, right feelings, right emotions, right choices, and right deeds, the body takes the command and acts accordingly. This will impact the cosmic vibrations. Then the universe will conspire to fulfill one's aspirations. Similarly, other humans will get impacted. Finally, the entire family, community, society and country will become a place of peace and harmonious living."

"Theoretically, it may be correct. But the reality is different. I am getting more and more confused. Is there any way to understand better?"

"The fear *is* the cause for the misunderstanding. According to Franklin D. Roosevelt "The only thing we have to fear is fear itself."

The fear of losing in competition plays havoc and the rest is only the mind's game. Whoever takes the plunge will never fail but succeed. This is the long story of human development and advancement in life.

Coming to the second conscious awareness, one can realize that it relates to the body. The body itself is the marvel of creation. The design, the architecture, the functions and the achievements are unique. In the words of William Shakespeare,

> "What a piece of work is man, how noble in reason how infinite in faculties; in form and moving, how express and admirable, in action how like an angel, in apprehension how like a god!"

This is a visible form of a treasure. This gift is the greatest treasure for the humans. The power of the physical strength of the body is enormous.

To be aware of the treasure—the body—safeguard it and put into use for the highest level of achievements is the challenge to humans. The best way is not to abuse, misuse and neglect it. One should find a way to love, nourish, discipline, and use for one's own self's fulfillment in life.

> "And your body is the harp of your soul, and it is yours to bring forth sweet music from it, or confused sounds."
>
> **Kahlil Gibran**

One should always take care of the body, which means not to abuse or misuse, or neglect it at any point of time. Terri Guillemets said that "Your body is a temple, but only if you treat it as one."

Each one should always adopt correct balance in food, drinks, eating, working, exercising and sleeping. Overdoing or under doing will harm the body and finally health.

Lastly, regarding the spirit it was said by Judith Light that "the body, mind, and the spirit are all connected. They are not separate pieces." The spirit is there in every one; it has to be identified and brought to light.

> "The spirit is the true self. The spirit, the will to win, and the will to excel are the things that endure."
>
> **Marcus Tullius Cicero**

Every human should always remember and continue to discipline and cultivate the spirit to take to magical pathways. They are imagination, dreams, intentions, present, beliefs, faiths, prayer, yoga and meditation, gratitude, humility, compassion, love, service, simplicity, appreciation, and spirituality.

When we go along on the *pathways,* we will be able to find them as solutions to the sufferings and pain which make many feel that life is real and painful.

Individually each magical pathway is not magical by itself. But when they are taken together to proceed regularly with constant focus and attention they all together get integrated and internalized in the body, the mind, and the spirit. The results of going on these magical pathways are magical. We therefore call them as magical pathways. These magical pathways will help one to get what one wants in life; peace, love, health, wealth, joy and happiness. Ultimately these pathways will lead everyone to magical life.

> "In oneself lies the whole world, and if you know how to look and learn, the door is there and the key is in your hands".
>
> **J. Krishnamurti**

Finally, the mind, the body and the spirit when in harmonious functioning will provide humans extraordinary powers to maximize their potentiality.

Achieving this in life should be the purpose which provides the meaning of life. Morihei Ueshiba once wrote that "everyone has a spirit that can be refined, a body that can be trained, in some manner, a suitable path to follow . . . ." It is therefore important for every human being to take care of the body, the mind, and the spirit to achieve what one wants to achieve in life.

> "If you nurture your mind, body and spirit, your time will expand. You will gain a new perspective that will allow you to accomplish much more."
>
> **Brian Koslow"**

"Thanks for your interesting and educative thoughts. I am truly benefited a lot. I would like to know whether the age will come in the way of following your magical pathways."

"No. Age, whether child, adolescent, adult, middle, or old, makes no difference. Everyone can follow the magical pathways irrespective of their ages. What is age?

It is a biological count by the numbers of years from one's date of birth. Numerically, we count the years by numbers. These magical pathways have to be identified and followed from childhood to the end.

Disciplined mind, the body, and the spirit are as important as food, air, and water for existence of life. Discipline means continuous practice of the mind, the spirit and the body.

In modern times, the word discipline sometimes is misunderstood as strict and difficult codes of conduct.

Also sometimes it is believed as an old fashioned idea with the connotation of religious or spiritual practice which will not fit in with the independent way of life in modern times whether child, young, adult or old. It is not true.

Simple discipline is concerned about good habits such as going to bed and getting up early to give the body and the mind required rest and relaxation for wellbeing; eating on time without over eating to avoid ulcers and obesity. Brushing and washing the teeth and the mouth after eating to avoid going frequently to dentists for treatments; doing yoga and meditation or exercises to keep the body and the mind fit; avoiding over stressful work or engagements to skip hypertension and heart problems, and so on. These are only a few examples. But they are simple and practical ways to live a healthy life.

In childhood, if children are taught by parents and in schools, they pick them up very well. The child's mind is always fresh and fertile to absorb any such practices and deeds. Slowly they get into their memory and get internalized. Once internalized, they become simple good habits. The habits then become their way of life. This will continue to happen when they become adolescent, adult, middle, and old. Beyond this, there is a mind and a soul.

If you think you are old at young age, you will become old at young age. If you, on the other hand, think that you are young at old age, you will become young at old age. This is what Elizabeth Arden said about age, "I am not interested in age. People who tell me their age are silly. You are as old as you feel."

Mark Twain said that "Age is a question of mind over matter. If you do not mind, it does not matter.

> "As a man thinketh in his heart, so is he."
>
> **The Bible**

Similarly, almost all philosophers, thinkers and writers echoed the same view on one's mind.

> "All that we are arises with our thoughts; with our thoughts we make our world."
>
> **Buddha**

The mind and the body are wired so intrinsically. 'What the mind commands, the body executes'.

The mind and body act may be with more than the speed of light. Once a famous circus trapeze artist said, 'I first put my mind on the bar, then the body follows automatically and I have easy flow of swing'. Age never comes in the way of achievers. George Bernard Shaw wrote a new play at the age of 82. Plato wrote 'The Laws' at the age of 83. Mother Teresa served the poor, destitute and sick and dying up to the age of 87.

Rabindranath Tagore was writing poems, dramas, and plays and making drawings at the age of 80. Pandit Ravi Shankar the sitar maestro gave his last performance in U.S.A. at the age of 92 just a few weeks before his death and he was given life time achievement award posthumously immediately in 2012. Jimmy Carter is serving the people globally through the Habitat for Humanity project at the age of 88. Bernard Shaw once wrote, 'the years in life matter less than the life in years'

"Is it not a strange argument?"

"No. If one has a conditioned mind, one will live in a conditioned environment."

"If so, why do many people withdraw from active work after 65 years or so?"

"Withdrawing from livelihood work does not mean withdrawing from life. It is only an end of one phase and at the same time beginning of another phase. When winter comes, it does not mean that all the seasons are over. Winter is followed by spring, spring is followed by summer, summer is followed by autumn, autumn is followed by winter again and the cycle goes on and on. Therefore, it is superficial to say that one is at his winter of his life or on his exit way of life."

"I am not able to understand clearly. May I request you to make it clear?"

"Life has seven stages: the baby, child, adolescent, and adult, middle, old and baby again. The baby grows into child, child grows into adolescent, adolescent grows into adult, adult grows into middle and middle grows into old. Till then, the growth goes on in an ascending order. Then there comes a quantum leap in reverse order. From old, the baby stage sets in at the end of one phase. This does not mean that an end has come.

Life never ends. It only changes its course in various phases. No beginning. No end. Life always moves in circles and cycles.

"While squares and rectangles have edges, circles do not have edges. If one has a conditioned mind, one can say that this can start from this point and end at another point. But in a circle once it is drawn, one cannot say where it starts and where it ends.

Among the seven stages, the adult, the middle and the old are very critical. Irrespective of what one learns as good habits in the childhood, when the adult stage sets in, one seeks pleasure and happiness all the time and finds no time to think and do good practices and good deeds. In the same way, in the middle stage, one runs after the work, money and family and finds no time to think and do good practices and good deeds.

Similarly, in the old stage, one lives in the past, ignoring the present and worrying about the future and the death and finds no time to think and do good practices and good deeds."

"My confusion is now compounded."

"If you think that you are confused, you are right. But if you have an open mind, you can understand. Closed mind closes all the doors of entry."

"What you mean by closed mind?"

"Closed mind means a mind that is conditioned by ego and self—pride. It keeps the mind in captivity and lives in a cocoon and does not allow one to learn and practice new ideas.

"I will try to keep my mind open and come back to you to proceed on the path if time permits. However, please tell me whether all these are original ideas?"

"There is nothing original in the world other than the Nature. Everything was there, is there and will be there. This is the perennial truth. Another thing, time will never permit, but it is always there. It is eternal. The question is how one should find it. I leave these thoughts with you to contemplate. When you come again, let us continue our search. Thanks for meeting me. Good day."

CHAPTER 2

Nature And Time

"Nature is man's teacher. She unfolds her treasures to his search, unseals his eyes, illumes his mind and purifies his heart; an influence breathes from all the sights and sounds of her existence."

Alfred Billings Street

"Time goes, you say? Ah no! Alas, time stays, we go."

Henry Austin Dobson

The young one met the old one and said,

"Last time we met, you left a thought with me to contemplate. You said that 'nothing but Nature is original'. Also, you said that 'time is eternal; but it is up to everyone to find it'. I tried to contemplate, but both appear to be elusive. Why is this so?"

"My dear friend, contemplation is not casual thinking. It is concentration with focus. If one does that, one will understand. You know Aristotle once said "Contemplation is the highest form of activity.""

"Let us take second one first. 'Time is eternal; but one should find it'. After all, what is time? Time is nothing but a concept. If the sun, the moon and the Earth do not orbit in the cosmos, there is no day or night. The concept of time would not have been evolved.

Time is eternal. But humans are temporary residents on Earth. Humans, however, evolved 24 hours in a day, 7 days in a week and 365 days in a year.

They always try to work within the boundaries they created for their existence and survival. These boundaries limit the activities and control the human existence on this lonely planet.

Humans therefore pushed into the fastest possible race and try to achieve as much as possible within the boundaries of time. Some call it rat race. Many get in to the trap knowingly or unknowingly. But millions get into it merely for existence and survival.

Most of their valuable life is wasted in adjusting their living within these boundaries. Day is for work and night is for rest. This is the way we trained our body and mind from time immemorial. But, due to advancement in science and technology particularly electricity, if one reverses this order continuously, the human body resists the change. This conflict leads to suffering and sometimes creates physical, mental and psychological problems. Finally, it manifests itself into ill health, family and social conflicts.

A U.K. scientific study published in 2012, in the journal *Bioessays,* says that "Over the past century, we have come to rely on electricity and begun staying up late. This forces us to go against our natural circadian rhythms, which throws off important hormones like melatonin, insulin, and cortisol." Other experts say that there is strong evidence that shift workers have higher rates of breast cancers, heart diseases, and diabetes.

Similarly, humans try to do one thousand things in one day whether connected or unconnected. They wisely call it as multiple multitasking. Many feel that everything will have to be done within a time frame even within a day or a week or a year. When the time is set for doing or achieving something or other, then the mind becomes a heavily loaded limb to activate the body.

According to them, time is measured and valued as money in the present day commercialized and monetized world. But the body and mind create conflicts between them. While the mind works non—stop, the body feels the pressure and strain. This conflict continues till some breakdown occurs either in the body or in the mind. Till then, humans work and exist without time even to think and reflect on themselves and the way they live their lives."

"Sorry. You seem to be going on a path that is not commonly traveled by everyone in this world. May I request you to slowly take me on your less-traveled path?"

"Before I completed the first part of your doubt, you have halted me straight in the middle. Anyway, I will try to continue and complete my answer. I assure you that I will go slow and take you along with me.

Now, coming back to your doubt, humans after seeing day and night, try to work within the boundaries they created for themselves.

Whenever they cross these boundaries, they face conflicts, ill-health, and sufferings.

Besides day and night, they also fall into time's trap of the past, present and future. In the words of Anais Nin "The past, present, and future mingle and pull us backward, forward or fix us in the present. We are made up of layers, cells, constellations." The past follows them like a shadow in the mind and this shadow threatens them and impacts them throughout their lifetimes and many times they bring sorrow and suffering. As far as the present is concerned, humans will never try to live in the present because of the impact of the past and the fear of the future. Regarding the future, humans live in the fear of the unknown.

The result is stress and strain all through one's life. To avoid this kind of misery, many thinkers have been repeatedly stressed the need for the humans to live in the present.

Dan Millman said, "The time is now and the place is here. Stay in the present. You can do nothing to change the past, and the future will never come exactly as you plan or hope".

Once a question was posed to His Holiness Dalai Lama and he replied in his own simple way. The question was: What thing about humanity surprises you the most? His answer was: "Man; because he sacrifices his health in order to make money, then he sacrifices his money to recuperate his health. And then he is so anxious about the future that he does not enjoy the present. And as a result, he does not live in the present or the future. And he lives as if he is never going to die and then he dies having never lived."

"It is very interesting to know how we all live. We have no time to think for ourselves about the precarious way we are living our life. But, as you know, when we face the reality in life, we have to keep pace with what is happening in the environment, society, and the world. Accordingly we are always pushed to exist on the edge and live our lives whether we like it or not. Is it not?"

"I am sorry. It is not true. One will have to first understand the nature of the perceived past, and the future. The past is dead and gone. But the shadow of the past insists to persist in the mind of the humans. Unless one changes the perception of the past with the aid of self realization which will come naturally to one who takes the magical pathways, it will as we see in everyone's life persists to stick around all the time.

The same is with the future. The future is unknown. Everyone knows as each one knows about the past. But threat is the peculiar feature of the future. Unless the threat perception is changed nothing will change. Magical pathways will help to deal with the situation.

The present is here in front of everyone. But everyone ignores. Why? The reason is simple. Everyone is entangled and overburdened with excess baggage of everything in every moment in life. Every moment counts in the Present. When moments are allowed to be slipped out of one's focus, then hours, days, and years will also get slipped and missed out for ever.

In the present, the choices available are infinite. Life, therefore, presents itself in the open arena with multiplicity of possibilities. It is up to anyone to take a correct path in the present and walk to the destination.

> "Time is a movement which man has divided into past, present and future, and as long as he divides it, he will always be in conflict."
>
> **J. Krishnamurti**

To avoid conflicts, one will have to learn not to live in the past. One cannot change the past as it has already happened and is lost. One should learn to let go the past. One should not entertain and nurture the memory of the past events; bad and harmful events or occurrences if nurtured will inflict more harm than actual incidents and lead to vicious circle of pain and sufferings. Also, one will have to learn not to fear the future. When the future is totally unknown, why should one worry about it? But the solution lies only in the present as it is eternal and presents itself to everyone in every moment in life. Alan Watts says that,

"Memories of the past and anticipation of the future exist only now, and thus to try to live completely in the present is to strive for what already is the case."

Eckhart Tolle in his book, 'The Power of Present' says that, "The division of life into past, present and future is mind-made and ultimately illusory. Past and future are thought forms, mental abstractions. The past can only be remembered now. What you remember is an event that took place in the Now, and you remember it now. The future, when it comes, is the Now. So the only thing that is real, the only thing there ever is, is the Now."

It is, therefore, necessary that one will have to live in the present—Now. All our wisdom traditions have repeatedly highlighted this aspect as a necessity for harmonious and peaceful life. In the field of science particularly the quantum physics the concept of time is known as vertical time. The past, present and future according to quantum physicists is nothing but an illusion. Einstein once said " .... that the distinction between past, present and future is an illusion, even if a stubborn one."

One day, I was sitting and watching humans in one mandapam (open hall with stone pillars) of about 1000 years' old temple. I was admiring the architecture, the beauty of the various stone sculptures, and the way the temple stood magnificently defying the ravages of 1000 and more number of years. All of a sudden a middle aged woman, Tulsi came and sat near me. She started saying that she had been seeing me talking to many people and that day she wanted to share with me something about her life. She said her life is full of pain and suffering. In short her life is painful. Some years back she happened to see a cruel car accident and her closest sister who was driving the car died on the spot. The trauma followed that accident deeply impacted her and never left her mind resulting in pain and enormous suffering. This had affected her work, relationships, personal life and financial matters and to say the least her life itself.

After listening to her story I suggested that there are certain pathways if she chose to take and follow through with regularity and commitment perhaps they would certainly mitigate her sufferings and pain. The pathway of meditation would help to reduce wandering mind and slowly still the mind. The pathways of intention, prayer, faith, love, service, and spirituality would help. Finally all these pathways would lead to the pathway of living in the present. If she followed these pathways strictly then her problems would be resolved. She listened carefully and took leave of me with confidence.

"I thank you for having patience with me and take me slowly on your path. But I still feel that the reality is different than what you are saying now. Everyone, including me, is so busy all through the day, night, week, month and year. Living in the present is not that easy as you suggest. Why is this so?"

"Yes. You may be right as long as you are not able to discriminate between what is needed now and what is not needed now. Socrates used to go to the markets to observe how people buy and live. One day, he told his friend that only after his regular visits to the market he realized how many things were there that he did not need.

One is always loading one's mind with unwanted and undesired thoughts. Accordingly, one always keeps his body engaged in unwanted and undesired activities. When the mind and the body are always kept excessively loaded, how can one find time? James Arthur Ray therefore said that "There are only two things you can do with time: spend it or invest it. If you spend it, is gone forever. When you invest your time, you will create a life time residual."

"What has that do to with one when one is not able to find time as one is always busy?"

"Busy with what? As I mentioned, one always lives with the clutter of unwanted excess baggage—physical, mental and material. This way, one creates one's own warehouse and says that one is always busy. Instead of one managing time, one allows time to manage him/her! This applies to many, but not to all.

My dear friend, you have to unload the excess baggage. This is simple. First, you have to 'let go' many memories that you carry in your mind unnecessarily. Also, one will have to keep clearing up material possessions and stop acquiring for the sake of acquiring. As far as physical activity is concerned, one should learn to draw a line between what is healthy for the body and what is not healthy for the body and act accordingly. Not one time. But one should do it continuously all the time.

Then one can find all the time in the world at one's disposal to invest it wisely and live a life of fulfillment."

"The butterfly counts not months but moments, and has time enough."
Rabindranath Tagore

"Yes. I will. But you should know that everyone is bombarded with so much news, advertisements, information, calamities, accidents, cinemas, serials, robberies and killings etc., every minute, day in and day out. Besides, one will have to attend to work, family children, travel, sickness, old age, pain, troubles, stress, strain, loss of loved ones, loss of friends, loss of companions and so many other things. What can one do with all these realities of today's life? That is why people say that they are always busy."

"You are right. If a dog bites a man, it does not become news. But if a man bites a dog, it becomes sensational news. More than that, most of them are invented manipulated, fabricated, paid, tutored to appear catchy, sensational, noisy, and appear to be real. News is not presented as pure news only. It is presented with a lot of make-up and dressing. They are always opinionated.

Information technology has helped to instantly throw up live news as and when they happen. Also by click of a button one can get enormous information on any matter in the world.

Explosion of information is the order of the day. This makes the existence complicated. All on line are neither authentic, nor useful for every human. One needs a lot of patience, intelligence, and time to get hold of the required correct information for one's needs.

Inducing, seducing, thrilling, and attractive video clips have become the way of modern marketing strategies in print and electronic media to catch and seduce the mind and heart of humans. Also multiple multitasking way of life has become normal in present times. When such things were not available, life was very simple. But other hardships crippled the humans at that time. One should not forget that one form of tyranny or other is repeatedly invading humanity. Present times, we are invaded by the tyranny of information technology.

But still there is hope. One should use the same knowledge age's techniques to discriminate between what is needed and what is not needed so that one can always unload unwanted excess baggage in any form. So practice prioritization of what you need and leave out all others. Do not always imitate others and do not try to do what others do. Imitation takes away human's originality and makes one as a slave of mediocrity."

"This is too much of a big dose of bitter medicine of advice for my age. I know you know many things. But I should make you understand that I am a young man. I also know that at your age I will be preaching these ideas to my youngsters at that time."

"Okay. This is the way the world is going around and around not only now but generations after generations in a circle of chains. Once at least, the chain should be broken. When humans realize that what they reserve to be understood and observed at the old age should be understood and practiced at the young age itself, then all will enjoy peace, health, happiness and longevity, which they aspire to acquire right now."

"Is it so? Please forgive me for my immature and impertinent reaction. I am trying to come out slowly of my old egoistic self-imposed arrogance. Please help me to the end."

"Realization is the first step towards spiritual journey. Don't worry. I will proceed from where we have halted. I am now pretty sure that from now onwards you will manage time and will never allow time to manage you. You should always be the master of your time and never be a slave.

Time and space are there forever. But humans forget that they are only temporary residents here. They erected boundaries of time and age within which they are trapped like lions in a cage. They keep pushing themselves and wandering within their own creations of small cages of their life. They yearn for freedom which becomes elusive till end. The magical pathways will provide the necessary tools to get out of the cages and enjoy freedom and happiness which will ultimately make life magical."

"Yes; of course. You said that nothing but the Nature is original. I feel that it is too simplistic statement. Humans also equally do original work. Is it not?"

"Nature is the mother of all creations. Nature is the sustainer. Nature is the dissolver. Nature is also the teacher, the guide and the philosopher. H.P.Blavatsky in her book, 'The Book of Golden Precepts' wrote, "Help nature and work on with her; and nature will regard thee as one of her creators and make obeisance. And she will open wide before thee the portals of her secret chambers, lay bare before thy gaze the treasures hidden in the very depths of her pure virgin bosom."

J. Krishnamurti wrote, that "When one loses the deep intimate relationship with nature, then temples, mosques, and churches become important." Such is the importance of the nature with the lives of all humans.

All originals therefore arise from one source i.e. Nature. The cosmos, the Earth, the sun, the moon, the stars, the galaxy, the oceans, the mountains, the rivers, the forests, the animals, the birds and the plants, all animate and inanimate things including humans are created by Nature.

From Darwin's Theory of Evolution to the modern Theory of Quantum Physics, all are attempts of human efforts to unveil the mystery of creation. The mystery still exists and the Nature continues to be supreme.

Nature is also a sustainer. It provides all that are essentials for life to exist and survive. The Earth, the water, the air, the fire, the sky, the oceans, the forests, the perennial rivers, the rains, the animals, the birds, the seasons, all other living creatures, animate and inanimate things including humans always provide ecological and biological balance and natural living conditions to each other for life to exist in our planet. All these keep systematically renewing and refreshing themselves on an on-going basis for the continuous existence of life system.

Nature is also dissolver. Even if one of its five elements shakes for a split second, the whole universe will shiver and suffer. Storms, earthquakes, thunder, tornadoes, torrential rains, snow and hottest seasons, famines, and epidemics are capable of throwing out of gear all humans' activities, and creations and inflicting injuries and deaths. The five elements identified and worshipped earlier days by humans such as earth, sky, water, fire and air are as powerful as ever.

All our scientific discoveries so far to a large extent are able to forecast in advance where, when and how these natural calamities may occur and warn people to take precautions. But still today the humans are not able to prevent those occurrences. Further humans cannot create Nature with all its originality, mighty power and abundance such as sky, oceans, cosmos, galaxy, sun, moon, rain forests, mountains, rivers, and other planets. Here lies the originality and the power of Nature. That is why I said that nothing but the Nature is original.

However, as long as humans appreciate the Nature and try to live as close as possible with Nature without excessive interference and exploitation then Nature will provide all the nutrients for healthy, happy, and wealthy life."

"Does this mean that humans are not creating and sustaining anything? Then what about the creation of art, literature, discoveries, inventions and a host of other things?"

"The artist creates a beautiful art of Mona Lisa or a sunset, sunrise, garden, forest, flower, mountain, river or whatever; he only creates a replica of the products and creations of Nature in one form or the other with his own imagination.

Take literature: the poet, the dramatist, essayist, novelist, story writer or whoever writes with his own imagination about the products and creations of Nature. Similarly take, discoveries and inventions, the scientists, explorers and adventurers, discover by their own efforts and intelligence the things that are already there, but unknown to the knowledge of humans till then.

Albert Einstein's view on natural law explains the superiority of nature in more effective terms. He said, that "The (scientists') religious feeling takes the form of a rapturous amazement at the harmony of natural law which reveals an intelligence of such superiority that, compared with it, all the systematic thinking and acting of human beings is an utterly insignificant reflection."

So nothing is original, including ideas, principles and even thoughts. But look at the paradox of life. An old story explains it in a very interesting way.

The story is . . .

'Once, a poor farmer was returning with his horse from the forest to his village. On the way, he saw a traveler from the city. The traveler was impressed by the beauty of the horse. He asked the farmer if he could paint the horse in his canvass. He also said that, for permitting him to paint, he would pay $5 to the farmer. The farmer thought that the whole day he could not get work for his horse and he could not earn any money and therefore he should accept the offer. He agreed and the traveler nicely painted his horse and made it a beautiful piece of art. The farmer took the money and happily went to his village.

After a few days, the farmer with his horse went to the city for some work. There in one market place was a big queue standing and buying tickets. He enquired and found out that some art show was going on and the ticket was $5. He had the money that the traveler gave him for painting his horse. He kept his horse outside and bought the ticket and went inside to see the art. To his surprise, the art piece was nothing but of his horse, which the traveler had painted some days before.

He caught hold of the traveler and said, 'this is nothing but a day light robbery. You made a painting of my horse on a canvass. This would not have cost you anything. But you were collecting huge money by exhibiting it as a great art. I could bring my horse and make it stand here real and with life. We both could collect more money and share it '.

The traveler told him that 'no one would pay for seeing a living horse and appreciate its beauty. They pay only for the art, which I have created on a canvass with life in it'. The farmer got annoyed and disappointed. He left the place and went away in disgust'.

This story is indicative of how humans are deluded by the replica of nature and they are slowly going away from appreciating and enjoying the original beauty of nature.

In the present monetized commercial way of life, every replica of nature is valued in terms of money, patented, registered and sold for money. This includes everything I said earlier.

We should understand the power and the impact of the nature on our earthly existence besides appreciating and enjoying the beauty and the enormity. The magical pathways will provide the necessary inputs to appreciate and enjoy the beauty and enormity of nature.

This in turn will make one's life enjoyable and peaceful. Then we will be in command of meeting the life's hardships and sufferings and make life magical."

"Thank you so much. I am slowly able to grasp. I am going to come to you again and again till you say goodbye for the good because I am now in command of my time."

"I am pleased. I am interested in leaving a thought with you to meditate. Is health the opposite of sickness? Is sickness a must or a choice in any age? Good day."

CHAPTER 3

Health

"Health is a state of complete physical, mental, and social well-being and not merely the absence of disease and infirmity."

W.H.O. Report

"*Good morning. It is a long time since I met you. Last time we met, you told me to meditate on two things before I come to you. One: is health the opposite of sickness? The other: is sickness a must or a choice? As usual, I tried. But I cannot boast to you that I am able to understand as I used to tell others. First of all, I am having a cart load of confusions about meditation in my head. Please clear my doubt first and tell me later about the other two questions?" the young one told the old one and waited for his reply.*

"Good morning. It is very nice to see you and talk to you. Yes; Meditation is one thing that has now become a commercialized product and often quoted as panacea for all sickness. I wonder whether you have time. If we talk about meditation, it might take a lot of time. Maybe, we may have to talk about it later."

"Yes, I agree. Time, as I told you earlier, is now my slave and not my master. Please, proceed."

"Yes; I used the word meditate. In simple terms it means 'to concentrate deeply with focus.' Let us take 'is health the opposite of sickness?' On the face of it, it sounds correct. But we have to find out what we mean by health. Health means, according to Oxford Dictionary, 'the condition of a person's body or mind'. James H. West defined "Health is a large word. It embraces not the body only, but the mind and the spirit as well . . . . and not today's pain or pleasure alone, but the whole being and outlook of a man."

A person may not have any sickness outwardly and he may look normal. But if he has a sick mind, how can we call him healthy? He himself may not know that he has a sick mind till it manifests in the body by way of some disease or pain. So, health is not necessarily the opposite of sickness."

"It looks to me again, as strange as you used to talk. We generally think that if any person looks normal, we take it for granted that he is free from sickness and therefore he is healthy. How can one find out that his mind is sick or not? Is there any way? You are very hypothetical and not practical."

"Wait. Do not come to any hasty conclusion. People generally believe that body and mind are totally different from each other. One does not have any connection with the other. Scientific research in the West proved that the ancient wisdom tradition's view that the body and mind are always connected was correct. In ordinary language, we can say that the mind is the motor of the body. It leads us to understand that the harmonious integrated functioning of both body and mind alone will lead to health. In the words of Buddha "Every human being is the author of his own health or disease."

"Health is a state of complete harmony of the body, mind and spirit. When one is free from physical disabilities and mental distractions, the gates of the soul open."

B.K.S. Iyengar

"You seem to pick up always unusual thoughts and highlight them as true, however much they are contrary to common beliefs and ways of living. Could you, for my sake, elaborate on this matter?"

"Of course, I will. The question, 'is health the opposite of sickness', itself assumes that sickness is inevitable and the mind revolves around sickness all the time, day after day, week after week, month after month, season after season, year after year.

If the mind is allowed to think of some sickness or other, the mind prepares the body to fall ill repeatedly on a regular basis on a set pattern. For example, eating out continuously will result in stomach upset, exposing to cold weather will bring sore throat, hard work will give headache, getting wet in rain will result in cold and fever, allergic problems will occur as and when seasons change and such other patterns of thoughts are somehow stored in the mind on account of childhood impressions, habits, and environmental influences.

The mind will always look out for some sickness or other as per the stored information and sickness will come as per correct schedules.

If you go to a doctor at that time, he will say due to the seasonal change, everyone is getting this kind of problem and a lot of patients have come to him with similar kind of sickness. Also, he will say that there is a virus infection all over the town or city."

"What you say is totally different from what is happening around us. What sickness has got to do with this kind of your imaginative theories?"

"Kindly be patient and I will clear your doubts. There is always another view for everything in this world. You may agree or may not agree. But nothing will be lost if one understands the other view as well. Also, not to be judgmental is a virtue."

"I am sorry. Please proceed. I will listen first and then ask my questions if I have doubts."

"What I am trying to say is the fundamental truth. If one keeps the mind free from rush, anger, jealousy, hatred, envy, greed, worry, anxiety, judgment, and the load of unwanted and undesired tit-bits of information on any subject, then the mind will become healthy. That kind of mind will enjoy freedom and protect the body as well from sickness and pain. If on the other hand one does not keep the mind free from those emotions and factors then the mind becomes unhealthy.

Take for example the case of anxiety which may look frivolous as other factors mentioned above but how it will affect the mental health is important to understand. In the words of Raymond Cramer "What does your anxiety do? It does not empty tomorrow of its sorrow, but it empties today of its strength. It does not make you escape the evil; it makes you unfit to cope with it if it comes."

All those emotions and factors are the root causes for the stress and strain one faces in daily life. These will slowly lead to headaches, which sometimes become chronic and may be finally diagnosed as migraine, high level of blood sugar, high blood pressure, finally ending up in eye-sight problems, foot problems and heart disease, body and joint pains, breathing problems and so on, finally leading to sickness, ill health and pains. Buddha's famous saying about the health of the body is that "To keep the body in good health is a duty . . . . Otherwise we shall not be able to keep our mind strong and clear."

Steve Maraboli said that "It is up to you today to start making healthy choices. Not choices, that are just healthy for your body, but healthy for your mind." Biological scientists say that the human life is revolving basically around two emotions, i.e. fear and love. If fear overtakes love, it affects the mind. This in turn inflicts diseases in the body. On the other hand, if love over takes fear, the mind will be totally free and healthy. This in turn makes the body healthy.

C.G.Jung, during the course of his practices on analytical psychology and psychiatry said that, "About a third of my cases are suffering from no clinically definable neurosis, but from the senselessness and emptiness of their lives. This can be defined as the general neurosis of our times." I would like to tell here, the conversation between the Doctor and Macbeth as it was written by the great poet William Shakespeare in his play Macbeth which explains vividly the problem of mental health which is so relevant even in our present times.

"Macbeth:How does your patient, doctor?

Doctor: Not so sick, my lord, as she is troubled with thick-coming fancies that keep her from rest.

Macbeth: Cure her of that! Canst thou not minister to a mind diseased, pluck from the memory a rooted sorrow, raze out the written troubles of the brain, and with some sweet oblivious antidote cleanse the stuffed bosom of that perilous stuff which weighs upon her heart.

Doctor: Therein the patient must minister to himself."

In this context, I remember what Hazrat Ali, a famous Sufi Master once said:

> "Your medicine is in you, and you do not observe it.
> Your ailment is from yourself, and you do not register it."

Hippocrates also emphasized the same fact in his own style. He said, that "Natural forces within us are the true healers of disease."

"Thanks. Now I could understand that the health is not necessarily the opposite of sickness. If anyone understands this fundamental truth, many of our minor ailments could be easily avoided. Now tell me about the other point. Is sickness a must or a choice?"

"I am glad that you could appreciate the truth. Coming to the next point, many of us always feel that sickness is a must. You know why? Because from childhood we are conditioned to think that sickness is always a must. As we discussed earlier, this is again the mind's game. When we have a conditioned mind that in childhood, adulthood and old age such and such sickness will befall us, then the mind invites sickness at the appropriate time and accordingly we keep falling ill as per the pre-arranged mind's schedules."

"I am sorry. This again appears to me that your imagination is running riot. I am not prepared to believe your theories anymore."

"I am not forcing you to agree with what I say. I am only trying to bring out the truths that are now scientifically proved by the scientists. If I say that these are our ancestor's views, you may not listen or agree. That is why I always say that the present modern scientists prove by their research that these truths are correct."

"I am sorry. I am trying to catch up fast. Please help me till I understand fully."

"If sickness is a must, the population of the world would not have reached the present explosive level. Secondly, there had never been adequate number of hospitals, doctors, and nurses to treat the sickness of the entire humanity at any point of time in the human history. If you take many underdeveloped and undeveloped countries even today the same position exists.

It is true that people fall sick. But it is not always a must. It is to a large extent mainly because of the choices which humans choose to make in day to day life. If you go to a doctor when you are sick, he first tries to diagnose to 'find out what the sickness is', and also to find out 'what is the immediate cause of the sickness'. Every other doctor diagnoses the sickness quickly. But the cause is difficult to find out immediately. He will ask for various investigations and tests to be carried out. Finally, the reports may say that there is high blood sugar, high blood pressure, high cholesterol, weak heart rate, and deficiency in calcium, potassium, in vitamins A to Z etc. But what caused these findings is far more important than the immediate treatment itself."

"I am now able to understand you. Please bear with me for my slow understanding."

"Thank you for understanding the truth. Now, coming back to those findings of the reports, you will find that the causes are mainly due to the choices one makes in day-to-day life. Choices of

eating habits
walking habits
talking habits
sleeping habits
drinking habits
smoking habits
working habits
breathing habits
exercising habits

"These simple, original, and existential habits have undergone a great deal of change due to the advancements in science and technology and the lifestyles humans have now adopted. Slowly, humans are going away from the natural environment and the natural living. When we say habits of that above nature one may think that these are all elementary and in the present fast, rapidly changing materialistic and mechanized knowledge age they carry no conviction or meaning to the present generation. These habits may look mundane but habits are very powerful and not only they never die but also become second nature. Also they not only shape but script the ways of life either for good or for bad.

Napoleon Hill said that "Habits are contagious. Every habit attracts a flock of its relatives." One can understand that good habits will attract other good habits. Similarly bad habits will keep on attracting other bad habits only and life may therefore revolve around only such bad habits if they are not checked and corrected in time. Seeing how such habits affect the humans, William Wordsworth was very angry when he wrote that, "Habits rule the unreflecting herd . . ."

> **"Nothing is in reality either pleasant or unpleasant by nature; but all things become so by habit."**
>
> **Epictetus**

"If you take eating, junk foods have multiplied and replaced healthy and natural foods. Humans now eat genetically modified foods. To meet the growing demands, food grains, poultry products, vegetables, fruits, meat and sea foods are genetically modified and manipulated by chemical fertilizers, insecticides, and artificial coloring agents. They all replaced natural products. To meet the rush in life, pre-cooked foods and even fully cooked foods of all kinds in attractive packages have replaced home-made foods.

As the readymade foods available in stores are made to look seductive, attractive and capable of inducing the taste buds to buy and eat on sight, the humans tend to eat more and more than actually required. In this context, it is very relevant to know how Philip J. Goscienski, M.D. in his book 'Health Secrets of the Stone age "links our modern dietary excesses to the rise in diseases that were rare until in the last century, including chronic diseases and the twin epidemics of obesity and diabetes."

Now the usage of organically cultivated grains, pulses, vegetables and other food products and food items and dairy and fishery products which are not genetically modified are gaining ground. But the progress is slow. Similarly the vegetarianism, dietary foods, and eating small portions of food at small intervals of time are getting popularized. These steps although progressing slowly may move fast and save humanity.

If you take walking, people rarely walk and rarely do exercise. Instead of natural exercises, humans use the machines to shake their limbs by rotation. One stands on a machine and the machine makes one walk on it. Regarding talking, people learn to live talking all the time. Mobiles, ear phones, face book, twitter, you tube, and blue tooth etc. are used day and night and also between the members of the family within the same house.

"One must be aware that all the machines and the electronic instruments such as treadmills, computers, laptops, mobiles, iPods, iPads, iPhones, T.Vs, music systems are all aids to betterment of life and not life itself. When these become all the time extended arms or organs of the body and the mind including the artificial intelligence, then they occupy all the spaces available for natural functioning of the organs, the body and the mind. Then the humans lose their heart and soul and tend to become machines like robots. Slowly the natural organs may give way and reshape themselves in different forms on the basis of evolution to cope with the newfound tasks which replaced old tasks.

Most of them emit a low level of radiation. The impact may be felt over time and not immediately. The more the humans get attached to the machines, the more they get detached from the other humans and the nature's life-giving nutrients. These aids if used excessively with obsession, they become addictions and make humans totally empty and lonely. When the choices and the options are not used on need based basis then the technology tend to make the humans as its slave. But the compulsions and seductions are very powerful and every human will have to be a part of the revolution. In the words of Stewart Brand, "Once a new technology rolls over you, if you are not part of the steamroller you are part of the road."

The homes from where the life blossoms have now become the store houses of computers and other electronics instruments, gym machines, liquor stocks, fast foods and medicines.

It looks that in future the planet mostly the cities and towns will be inhabited mostly by human robots and the machine robots without human feelings, ethos, emotions, empathy, love, affection and sympathy. In this context one should take note of the warning given by Arthur C.Clarke that, "Before you become too entranced with gorgeous gadgets and mesmerizing video displays, let me remind you that information is not knowledge, knowledge is not wisdom, and wisdom is not foresight. Each grows out of the other, and we need them all."

The love, family celebrations, closeness of the families and relatives, small pleasures of drinking, eating together and togetherness of everyone in the family, sharing joy and sorrow together, sharing happiness and achievements with others and helping others and enjoying their achievements, social and community gatherings are slowly vanishing and may become non—existent over a period of time. If this happens then the life will become a totally self-centered, hollow, lonely, and empty.

When you take sleeping, people surrounded by modern gadgets do not get sleep at all. Multiple modern gadgets such as music system, home theatre, lap tops, face book, you tube, blue tooth, e-books, mobiles etc keep humans engaged till mid night and sometimes all through the nights. Once this habit becomes addiction then it will never die. Multi-billion-dollar businesses of sleeping pills alone make people to go to sleep. Research and health studies now reveals that although these pills provide sleep and help to get quick relief overtime the accumulated toxins lead to memory loss and Alzheimer's problems.

If you take drinking, most humans slowly tend to neglect to drink water and instead drink beer and liquor all the time. Drinking natural water is slowly getting vanished. Such humans if at all take water they drink only chemically treated water in the name of mineral or packaged water. These chemicals accumulate toxins in the body and over time lead to different kinds of health problems.

Smoking has become a minute to minute ritual of living. Smokers inhale and exhale smoke. The smoke burns the lungs with every inhaling of smoke. It affects other people's lungs with every exhaling of smoke which they call passive smoking. This is the most deadly addiction which catches the young humans in schools, work places to start with as fun by peer level pressures and finally ends up as untreatable addiction.

Addictions to alcoholism and smoking are the two major causes of deaths of valuable lives of humans. This happens in every second in every part of the world due to cardiovascular diseases, killings, and accidents. Besides, these two are the major causes of killings, fights, family disruptions, social tensions, developing anti-social elements in society and become the sources of many other evils in the society.

As far as working is concerned, people have not only become stress givers, but also suffer serious stress and strain themselves. As per scientific studies tensions are the number one cause for many health problems of humans.

People also inhale and exhale only conditioned air. Breathing in natural fresh air has gone out of our living either in the day or in the night. Breathing is natural. But due to the stressful life style one leads now, people have adopted shallow breathing. Sun light is an essential ingredient for healthy body and mind. But humans closed all the doors of getting natural sun light in daily existence. Scientists now say that insufficient exposure to sun light results in the spread of cancers.

Exercise is the second important aspect for the healthy existence of life next only to breath. When breath comes naturally for existence the exercise will have to be undertaken by the humans. In the baby stage the baby kicks, makes noises, and cries automatically to grow by her own way. But from the child stage onwards it will have to be undertaken by the child, adult, middle and old age. In the olden days humans required to walk long distances and do a lot of manual and physical work. This kind of living had taken care of exercises by their living styles.

But in the modern life styles of the humans, unless special efforts are taken for allotting time and doing exercises, humans tend to ignore exercises very conveniently for want of time. Humans never realize the importance of exercises till obesity, diabetes, high blood pressure, and other manifestations of diseases strike them unexpectedly at the height of their so called busy life with full of never ending activities. The pity is that living in the internet age everyone knows almost every aspect of healthy living. Still living blindly ignoring exercises may be a mystical aspect of many in this modern age.

"You seem to have touched the core point of the present human existence. But you have made it so brief that I may miss many of your valuable thoughts. May I request you to elaborate on these points for my benefit?"

"We have talked about how the mind and the body get influenced and affected by the choices one makes in the day-to-day life out of the infinite choices of modern lifestyles that have been made available by the developments in science and technology. However, one will have to learn to love, nourish and sustain the body, the mind and the spirit.

It all depends how one uses or misuses or abuses the body, the mind and the spirit. If they are put into optimal level of healthy uses, most of the health problems could be avoided. If one makes the right choice at the right time, the sickness could by and large be avoided. It is reported in research studies that ninety five per cent of the sicknesses could be avoided if one makes the correct and healthy choices in adopting the various nine habits we discussed earlier.

> "Five per cent of all diseases today stem from single gene disorders, whereas around ninety five per cent of all illnesses are related to life-style choices, chronic stress, and toxic factors in environment".
>
> **Dr. Joe Dispenza**

Therefore, sickness is mostly by choices one makes in day to day life. As far as the spirit is concerned besides what we have already discussed one will have to identify, nurture, and cultivate and choose a spiritual path to lead a healthy life.

"I must ask you one more question. Is there any other matter about which one should be careful for ensuring good health?"

"Yes. What we discussed is concerned with the body, the mind and the spirit of the individual. The solution, therefore, lies with the individual. But there are external factors too, which play vital role in an individual's health. They are the environment, living conditions, pollution of all kinds and increasing interference of humans with Nature and it's functioning.

"Our planet is the only planet in which life exists. Scientists are still searching for life in other planets. Our planet is the provider and sustainer of life. Five basic elements i.e. earth, water, fire, air and ether help humans to have life and live. But unfortunately, with recklessness and mindlessness, in the name of industrialization, commercialization, explorations, development, scientific investigations and modernization, humans are constantly exploiting the nature.

The underground, on the ground, and underwater atomic tests, underwater explorations and atomic power generations of every country interfere with the natural functioning of the nature in its own way. These with other kinds of explorations, and industrialization, have resulted in the pollution of air, water, earth, sky and every other matter that nature has provided for safe and healthy living in the planet.

It is brought out in various scientific studies that due to all these factors the glaziers in mountains are melting, the water level in the oceans are rising; the coastal areas near the seas are being swallowed by rising sea water levels and the sea water is getting warmer and warmer year after year. In addition, the waste such as industrial waste, nuclear waste, electronic products' waste, satellites' debris falling from skies and chemical waste etc. pollute the planet with unprecedented impact with threatening consequences on human existence itself."

"Is it not frightening? Is there any salvation from man's creation of his own problems?"

"The pollution and exploitation of the natural resources impact the planet in a very serious manner. The planet starts sending various kinds of warning signals in the form of hurricanes, tornadoes, earthquakes, tsunamis, heavy snow falls, draughts, forest fires and severe heat conditions. These natural calamities are now occurring with more severity and more frequency than ever before in human history.

Hurricanes Katrina in 2005 and Sandy in 2012 were the deadliest and most destructive storms. They devastated coastal areas of U.S.A.

including New York and New Jersey etc. Millions were evacuated, rendered homeless and power supply was not available for more than three days. Similarly the tsunami of 2004 after the severe earth quake struck under the sea in Sumatra, Indonesia have inflicted enormous devastation in Indonesia, Thailand, Sri Lanka and India and other coastal areas of other South East Asian countries. Chernobyl atomic power plant's accidental explosion in Russia and Fukushima Atomic power plants explosion in 2011 caused by powerful earthquake and tsunami in Japan are the pointers to the dangers of nuclear power plants.

It is reported that in U.S.A, a resolution saying that "climate change is occurring, is caused largely by human activities and poses significant risks for public health and welfare" was placed before the congress in 2011. Although it was not passed for want of majority votes, it indicates the enormities of the problem created by the humans and signify the urgency of taking preventive proactive measures.

After the worst ever earthquake and tsunami devastated three atomic power plants in Fukushima, Japan which resulted in radiation spreading all over the nearby areas in 2011, people all over the world are now worried about the safety of the existing and the future atomic power plants. When these incidents occur, they destroy the natural resources, human lives and continue to affect the future generations with severe radiation problems.

The head of a renewable energy think tank in Germany said on

26th May 2012 that German solar power plants have produced a world record 22 giga-watts of electricity per hour equal to 20 Nuclear power Stations at full capacity—through the midday hours on Friday and Saturday. The German government decided to abandon nuclear power after the Fukushima nuclear disaster in 2011, closing eight plants immediately and shutting down the remaining nine by 2022 (Reuters).

Presently, the countries are talking about food security, water security, green gas effect, climate change and global warming. Japan has planned to shut down all the nuclear power plants within a period of twenty five years. During this period they will make all out research programmes to find alternate power resources such as solar, geothermal, bio fuel, and wind, hydrogen energy etc.

France has decided to replace the nuclear power by other alternative sources of power in due course. Switzerland has decided the same way. U.S.A is not going in for new nuclear power plants. But some of these countries are now exporting nuclear power plants to underdeveloped and developing countries assuring safety and undertaking re-processing of nuclear waste effectively.

Dr. Hans-peter Duerr, is a German Physicist and Nobel Peace laureate. In the 1950s he worked as a student under Edward Teller, considered the father of the hydrogen bomb, before turning a peacenik and staunch opponent of nuclear reactors. He is a Director Emeritus, Max-Planck Institute for physics, Germany.

On the 8th. March 2012 he said: "Nuclear energy could never be a safe or sustainable option for mankind and any claims to the contrary were nonsensical. While it was impossible to completely vouch for the safety of a nuclear reactor, even if one worked out safeguards for imagined threat scenarios, nuclear waste and its safe disposal was an even bigger problem. In fact nuclear waste in the wrong hands could be used for making atom bombs.

The dangers may appear to be of no immediate concern. But the health and life of the future generations may have to be mortgaged for the present convenience of enjoying power from nuclear power plants.

The solution lies in how far humans safeguard themselves by their timely preventive actions. Hopefully in this century humans will find solutions to these problems with their ingenuity and scientific quantum leap jump in knowledge development."

"It looks to me like we are in a critical crossroad of human existence on the planet. Are there quick solutions to all these problems?"

"Yes, you are right. All the countries in the world have now realized the immediate necessity of finding solutions to these problems. You know that these problems are created by humans. Now they have to change their mind set from the earlier mind set of exploitation of nature to the preservation of nature. It is, therefore, up to them to find solutions from a different perspective.

> "No problem can be solved from the same level of consciousness that created it."
>
> **Albert Einstein**

"It is, therefore, important that extraordinary measures are to be taken on a global basis. It is no longer an individual country's problem. It is a problem of human existence in every country and it has, therefore, become a global problem. If all countries come together with global consciousness, they can find the solutions. This is the hope of humanity in this century.

"Similarly, if individuals conscientiously keep the awareness of health at every stage in life, the entire society's problems may be resolved. In human life, health is critical in every stage of life. Whatever they sow at these stages of life, they will reap in later parts of their lives. If they sow good seeds, they will reap good harvests. On the other hand, if they sow bad seeds, they will reap bad harvests. The seeds are their thoughts, words, choices, actions and habits. In this context the magical pathways will help everyone irrespective of age to make one's life magical."

> "Watch your thoughts; they become your words.
> Watch your words; they become your actions.
> Watch your actions; they become your habits.
> Watch your habits; they become your character.
> Watch your character, for it will become your destiny."
>
> **Hillel**

"But many live their lives as if nothing will happen. Even if some bad thing like losing health happens, they always feel that it can be treated and restored later. After sickness and suffering, if they regain their lost health, they generally feel happier than before. An old story comes to my mind.

There was a very rich man in a town. Although he had everything in life, he felt unhappiness with everything he was doing. He, therefore, decided to travel with a full bag of diamonds in search of some master who could show him the way to bliss and happiness and present the bag of diamonds to him if he showed the way. He met a Sufi on the way and offered the bag of diamonds and requested him to show him the way to bliss and happiness. Sufi grabbed the bag and ran away.

The rich man chased him, but he could not catch the Sufi. After hearing his cries, the men in the town gathered and went into all the streets of the town in search of the Sufi. They also could not find the Sufi. The rich man lost all hope. He, therefore, decided to return home with his heart broken. On his way, he saw the same Sufi sitting under a tree. He also saw his diamond bag was lying by his side.

Immediately, he went near the Sufi and took back his lost diamond bag. The Sufi asked him if he is happy now. The rich man said he is happier than before. The Sufi told him that this is the key for bliss and happiness. The rich man, with his newfound happiness, went home."

"The story is very interesting. Losing one's health and regaining after suffering is like the rich man giving away the diamond bag and getting it back feeling happier than before. I must thank you for your time and elucidation. Still, I have one doubt. Why do people, even if they make correct choices and live satisfied and good lives in the best of living conditions such as health and wealth get serious sickness?"

"Good, you raised this very important point. I would, therefore, leave a thought with you: 'is karma the cause for the suffering and sickness of people?' Please reflect on this point. When we meet again, we will put our thoughts together and try to find the truth. Good day.

CHAPTER 4

Karma

My actions are my only true belongings.
I cannot escape the consequence s of my actions.
My actions are the ground upon which I stand.
Thich Nhat Hanh

"*Good morning. I am sorry for not meeting you for a long time, as I was away on an official tour.*" *The young one was apologetic when he met the old one.*

"I am glad that you remembered me and came today."

"*Last time we met, you asked me to reflect on: is karma the cause for the suffering and sickness of people? Even on tour, I reflected on karma. I realized that karma conveys different meanings to different people. As usual, I am confused. Could you please make me understand correctly?*"

"You are right. Karma is a word which is often loosely and wrongly used in day-to-day conversations by people. Whenever a person is sick and suffers seriously, people will say that it is due to his karma. On the other hand, whenever a person is doing well in his life, people will never say that it is due to his karma. This only shows that people generally relate the word karma to sickness or suffering I mean extraordinary in both cases. But they will not relate it with happiness or health. The reason is very simple. When people are healthy and happy they will never try to understand why that has happened to them. But when the same people face sickness or suffering they will try to understand why such things happened only to them. The reason is to get cure or relief from such inflictions.

There are certain things in life that cannot be changed, for example, aging, sickness, suffering, pain, natural calamities and death. The causes for such things cannot be easily understood by people. Therefore, they try to explain them away by means of certain unknown or incomprehensive theories. The theory of karma is one such theory."

"There are some more happenings in human life for which neither the philosophers nor the scientists could still find answers. In the same family living in the same environment some children are born with infirmity, and some with very little intelligence and some with deformity. Again some get three to four babies in one delivery and in some cases no baby at all. Similarly even those live in the most ideal healthy conditions get incurable diseases and suffer.

Accidents happen and people suffer and die. Epidemics in unknown forms suddenly erupt and kill humans however much they try to control and prevent such incidents. In the case of natural calamities scientists forecast in advance the nature and severity of such events. But they still could not prevent such occurrences. Alleviative measures and explanations are made available only after such events take place. What are the causes for these occurrences? Do you mean to say that the karma is the cause? If not are these acts of God?"

"These are mystical aspects of Nature's part played out in human life. Here I am talking about the theory of karma. Any theory, for that matter, reflects the human mind's exploration of God's mysterious ways of creation and its ways of functioning relating to the time and period in which the humans lived or living. This includes the functioning of the universe or the lives of humans or the inter-relationships between them. This happens with a saint or yogi or poet or writer or scientist or philosopher reflecting the conditions prevailing in a particular period of time in which each one of them lived or lives."

"I am sorry to say that I am still confused. Is there any way to understand easily?"

"My dear young man, there is no short cut to knowledge. If you want to understand correctly, you may have to exercise your mind. Maharishis, rishis and seers of ancient times used their minds' eyes as instruments to explore the mind's functioning as well as the functioning of the universe. Also, they explored the mysterious ways of God's creation.

They tried to understand the purpose and the meaning of human life on Earth, the duality of the very existence of human life with suffering and happiness. They exercised their mind to find a way to end the suffering. They were able to transcend the time and space by their powers of mind. At this point, they realized that the human life is a continuous process of birth and rebirth. This led them to discover that the law of nature operated on the basis of cause and effect even in human life.

"Every action in thought, word and deed creates a reaction in life. If you throw a small stone on the still water of a big lake, it will create a ripple that multiplies by itself and goes on and on till you again throw another stone. This is the way the thoughts in the mind and the theory of karma works.

In other words, it works by means of cause and effect and action and re-action. In this process, the mind plays a vital role in human life.

> "Cause and effect, means and ends, seed and fruit, cannot
> be severed; for the effect already blooms
> in the cause, the end pre-exists
> in the means, the fruit in the seed . . .
> you cannot do wrong without
> suffering wrong."
> **Ralph Waldo Emerson**

"Thank you for taking me to the right path. May I know now if all religions believe in karma? Also, who was the first to comprehend the theory of karma?"

"I appreciate your investigative mind. This is one of the steps to climb the spiritual path. All major religions that believe in re-birth accept the theory of karma in one form or other. Hinduism identified the nature of karma in the lives of humans. This, as other codes of good conduct of human behaviors and the individual's patterns of lives with suffering and happiness was preserved and passed on from generations to generations from time immemorial only by the word of mouth. Later, they were codified in the Upanishads, Vedas, and Bhagavad-Gita and other scriptures.

"Till date no one could establish the origin of this theory. Christianity believes in re-incarnation, heaven and hell. Islam believes in after life paradise or fire, for the actions during one's life. Buddhism believes in re-birth. Jainism also strongly believes in re—birth. Jainism also strongly believes in karma. If you study closely all religions, their main objective is to inculcate good conduct in human lives. To ensure this code of conduct, reward and punishment for the good and bad conducts respectively were brought about through the theory of karma. 'As you sow, so shall you reap' and 'what goes around comes around'. This is the way the theory of karma works according to many faiths."

"Is it derived from the study of human lives only to explain the reason for the serious sickness, and sufferings in as much as such things happen in the lives of humans in every generation after generation without any exception?"

"You are absolutely right. In Sangam Age (300 BC to 300 AD) a literary period of Chera, Chola and Pandya kingdoms in the Southern India, now called Tamil Nadu, the famous Tamil poet, Kaniyan Poongkundranar, wrote:

"Every country is my country; everyone is my relative.
Bad and good are not given by others;
suffering and happiness come on their own.
Death is not new; never feel happy
thinking life is full of happiness,
never feel unhappy,
thinking life is full of suffering.
Lightning followed by skies'
small drops of rain collect
into noisy falls coming down
from the slopes of the mountains
to plains and runs as rivers,
life as a float, floats in their waters
as per its own nature it goes
wherever the flow of water goes
This, learned ones know,
therefore, never wonder about
great and never despise small people."

"Gautama Buddha echoed this phenomenon as follows:

"Events happen, deeds are done, consequences happen, but there is no individual doer of any deed."

"Thiruvalluvar, a secular poet of Sangam Age, wrote about karma in Chapter 38, containing 10 two line aphorisms in his Thirukkural.

Poet Elango Adigal of Sangam Age crafted his epic Silappathikaram around the play of karma and its effects on the lives of Kovalan and Kannagi, the main characters in the epic. He is emphatic in his assertion that karma will impact the lives of everyone with its full force in everyone's life time.

"Even the Avatars of God, once they have taken a birth as humans on Earth, were not spared from the clutches of karma. Rama and Karna are classic cases. Any sage, rishi, yogi, rich, poor, king, mighty, rulers, subjects and everyone in life is subjected to this unknown phenomenon. In recent history, the spiritual leaders Ramana Maharishi and Ramakrishna Paramahamsa had to face sickness, but with a difference from ordinary humans. As they were sages, sickness did not bring them suffering. They treated pain as inevitable and suffering as choice with the result the sickness did not affect them at all as it affects ordinary humans."

"If karma is such a powerful phenomenon, why then, do people talk about destiny, fate and luck? If destiny decides someone's sickness or sufferings in this life, what does karma, whether it is past karma or present karma, do about it? In the same way, if fate decides someone's sickness or sufferings in this life, how will the theory of karma work? Are destiny and fate determined only by the theory of karma? Or does each one nullify the effect of the other?

To add more to my confusion, people also say when someone is doing extremely well in this life that his luck has brought him success and happiness. Here, luck always pre-supposes happiness. It appears that if one has luck, it nullifies the effect of bad karma, which is supposed to bring only sickness and sufferings. If someone loses his health, wealth, or fails in his efforts, people say that it is his bad luck. I am now in the midst of total confusion. Could you please salvage me from my delusion by your wisdom?"

"These are simple words. But when used in out of context, they will certainly throw up confusion. Destiny and fate convey more or less the same meaning. The word destiny is generally used by people to describe the reason for the happenings in one's life.

Maharishi Vashistha, at the insistence of Maharishi Valmeeki, in his discourse to Shri Rama described the fate in a full chapter. He says: 'there is nothing called fate. Fate does not exist. Fate is ever unreal'.

The sage goes on to say using very strong words to denounce the very word fate. He concluded finally that: **"There is nothing called fate which has a form other than one's own former action. That former human effort is indeed described by the word fate."** **The Vision and the Way of Vasistha**

"As far as luck is concerned, people say 'good luck' when they convey good wishes to someone. But when someone fails to achieve something, people say that it is his 'bad luck'. Therefore, karma has nothing to do with these words."

"What you have been saying so far may be a philosophical view of karma. Has science ever accepted karma even as a theory?"

"Philosophy and science have so far been considered as two parallel lines that will never meet. Philosophers considered science as one without soul. Scientists considered philosophy as one without verifiable evidence. Your question itself conveys your feeling that science will never accept the theory of karma. It was true till 19th century. After Einstein proclaimed his Special Theory of Relativity and later his General Theory of Relativity, followed by Unified Quantum Field Theories and the Theory of Uncertainty, scientists started echoing the ideas of ancient Upanishads and Vedas.

The quantum physics scientists now come close to the ancient concepts of seeing whatever appears as solid is not solid but only waves of vibrations.

John Wheeler, a theoretical physicist, said, 'the universe does not exist unless there is a conscious observer'.

Also, it is said that quantum physics shows that reality is not concrete at all and that deterministic scientific laws are no more than mathematics of probability.

All these scientific findings echo the age-old Vedic concepts such as unified consciousness—supreme spirit—Agham Brahmasmi. In short, matter is nothing but energy; energy is only thought and thought is only a vibration on the surface, so to speak of the calm ocean, the Supreme Spirit."

"I am sorry to say that my confusion now got compounded. What you say, to my mind, has nothing to do with my question i.e. whether science has accepted the theory of karma or not?"

"Whether the science accepts the theory of karma is one thing and whether the theory of karma, which is based on philosophy and religion, can be verified and acceptable to everyone is another thing. What I am trying to say is that the scientists of modern age by their own scientific discoveries are slowly coming closer to the ancient ideas of philosophy and religion. If you have patience, which is a rare commodity in the modern rat race world, I will lead you to the correct perspective of karma."

"I am very sorry for my impatience. Please bear with me and help me to go with you."

"It is okay. The great scientist, Albert Einstein, once said, 'Science without religion is lame; religion without science is blind'.

"However, starting from Aristotle, till today, the great thinkers of the human race are still striving hard to find answers for human actions that lead to sickness and sufferings. Aristotle said the following.

"All human actions have one or more of these seven causes:

> *chance*
> *nature*
> *compulsions*
> *habit*
> *reason*
> *passion*
> *desires"*

These seven causes by and large lead humans to act in one way or other. Such actions alone will bring either happiness or sufferings as per their individual nature. Good chance will lead to good results. Similarly bad chance will have opposite result. This applies equally to all the other six causes. But the fundamental action lies only in the hands of humans. Therefore one can say that the choices one makes in life under any one of these causes will alone bring either sufferings or happiness in one's life and not karma as an unknown phenomenon.

"Sigmund Freud, Carl Jung and other New Age writers have expounded different theories based on psychology, sociology, psychiatry and neurology such as the Theory of Intentionality, Theory of Synchronicity and Theory of Chance and Theory of Attraction. All of them in one way or other are trying to explore the reasons for sickness and sufferings and also the ways and means to eliminate them as far as possible.

"Some of the modern psychologists and modern medical scientists are trying to scientifically understand the rebirth and how the past acts of individuals in their earlier births impact their present life particularly with sufferings.

They are also using the methods of regression and progression to heal the sufferings and looking into the future births.

The noted psychiatrist, Dr. Brian L. Weiss, M.D., says, "As we have had limitless past lives, so will we have limitless future ones. Using our knowledge of what went before and what is to come, we may be able to shape the world's future and our future. These ties into the ancient concept of karma. What you do, so shall you reap. If you plant better seeds, grow better crops and perform better actions, your harvesting in the future will reward you".

We can conclude saying that by altering the attitudes, changing the lifestyles, following magical pathways particularly such as love, compassion, loving kindness, prayer, yoga and meditation, and spirituality in one's life, one can escape the severe impact of karmic effects in the present life itself, if at all there are any such phenomenon. I must conclude with the words of William James, the modern philosopher of America,

"The greatest discovery of my generation is that a human being can alter his life by altering his attitudes of his mind."

Finally, whatever we may try to understand about some of those mystical parts of human life whether they happen due to karma or not the fact remains that major parts of the human life lies only in the hands of humans themselves.

"Life is 10% of what happens to me
and 90% of how I react to it."

John Maxwell

"I must thank you for your elaborate exposition on karma. I am greatly indebted to you. May I take leave of you now, only to meet you soon to proceed further on our journey?"

"Thank you so much for your patience. When we meet again, let us put our thoughts together on 'religion and spirituality'. Good day."

CHAPTER 5

Religion And Spirituality

"Spiritual wants and instincts are as various in the human
family as are physical appetites, complexions and features,
and a man is only at this best normally, when he is equipped
with the religious garment whose color and shape and
size most nicely accommodate themselves to the spiritual
complexion, angularities and stature of the individual who
wears it."

Mark Twain

"**G**ood morning. It is nice to see you today."

*"Good morning. I am blessed to be here today. Last time I met you,
you asked me to ponder 'are religion and spirituality the same or opposite
of each other.' I spent a lot of time and ended up in utter confusion,"* the
young one told the old one.

"I understand your predicament. It is a complex matter. Each one looks at
it differently from the other. The truth is always buried under the debris
of misunderstanding and ignorance. It is better to understand what we
mean by religion and spirituality. There are two meanings for any word.
One is literal and the other is popular.

The religion literally means the belief in a God or gods and the activities
connected with this. But in popular understanding it is practiced as
exclusiveness of rituals with or without genuineness of faith in the
name of particular God or gods. Also the moral values and ethical codes
of conduct of the religion or religions in humans' lives are slowly being
ignored and more importance is being given for the outward rituals to
appease the God or gods.

Spirituality literally means having deep thoughts, feelings or emotions rather than the body or physical things and belief in God.

But in popular understanding it is always regarded as part of any religion or religions and all the rituals attached to the religion or religions with either total or partial denouncement of earthly life are considered as spirituality.

Humans are spiritual beings of various religions or no religion. Religion comes by birth. If one is born into a Christian family, one becomes a Christian. If one is born into a Muslim family, one becomes a Muslim. Similarly, it applies to everyone whether one is Hindu, Jew, Sikh or any other religion. Spirituality comes with the body. A spiritual person may or may not belong to a religion. But all religious people are spiritual in nature. But most may not have spirituality as the core aspect of their life."

"May I interrupt? You mean to say that only through rituals many humans practice religion or religions. "

"I will put it in another way. Rituals have become more important than genuine faith or belief in God or gods for many people. The rituals are done as a trade-off. They are done only to obtain what one wants to obtain in return. Simple and genuine prayers are side-lined. Extravagant and expensive rituals are being considered as the best way to get God's blessings. Why this has happened is a big question. If you have patience and time, we may look at it in a historical perspective."

"Please proceed. I have now come a long way. I will certainly pay attention and give time for whatever you say."

"Good. Starting from the Stone Age to the present Knowledge Age, mystery of the unknown played an important role in human life. The mystery of the universe and the ways the five elements i.e. fire, water, earth, air and ether functioned gave rise to bewilderment and fear in the minds of the humans. They started worshiping the five elements as gods. Also, they thought that they are the manifestations of some unknown supernatural power, which made them work as well as all other living and non-living things in the universe. They invoked them to keep the people safe, healthy and in peace.

"They also realized by experience that with the body there is something that makes them see, touch, smell, taste and hear.

Beyond these five natural physical powers, called five senses, the humans in their evolutionary process realized that there are emotions, feelings, remembrances, thoughts, realizations, empathy, sympathy and relationships in their day-to-day life. This is where everyone is connected with the spirit, which finally leads one to realize the aspect of spirituality.

The organized religions one after the other was founded in the course of human history. These religions laid emphasis on the omnipotent, omnipresent and omniscient nature of God. Also, they laid emphasis on good conduct and behavior. They laid down practices and procedures for correct ways of living, worship, prayer and rituals. Religion also came to regulate men's lives through their moral and ethical laws.

Even in the modern scientific age, the religions play unshakable role in the lives of the people. It is reported that in one of the Gallop Polls conducted in the year 2006 in U.S.A. ninety four per cent said that they believe in God and eighty two per cent said that religion is important for them.

One should remember that religions have evolved over time on the beliefs, faiths and the strong mental attachments. The present day neuroscientists discovered that the human brain by itself evolved to have a small center in everyone's brain which they call it "god's spot'.

It is reported that the neurophysiologist Dr. Michael Persinger and neurologist Dr. V.S. Ramachandran carried out research on the human brain which led them to understand the existence of 'god spot' in the human brain. It is said that the 'god spot' does not prove the existence of God, but it does show that the brain has evolved over time to ask eternal questions to find out wider meaning and value in life.Besides, other scientists also acknowledge that the moral standards and ethical values arising out of religious teachings have played important roles in the lives of the humans.

Albert Einstein wrote that "Our time is distinguished by wonderful achievements in the fields of scientific understanding and the technical application of those insights. Who would not be cheered by this? But let us not forget that knowledge and skills alone cannot lead humanity to a happy and dignified life. Humanity has every reason to place the proclaimers of high moral standards and values above the discoverers of objective truth, what humanity owes to personalities like Buddha, Moses and Jesus rank for me higher than all the achievements of the inquiring and constructive mind."

"Sorry for my interruption. You mean to say that every religion was evolved in a similar way?"

"In fact, every religion, i.e. Hinduism, Buddhism, Jainism, Christianity, Islam, Judaism, Sikhism, Zoroastrianism, Baha'ism, Sufism, Taoism and Confucianism etc. lays down emphasis on spirituality and the ways to gain spirituality in one's life. It is important to know briefly about the various religions' basic concepts and core teachings."

HINDUISM

Hinduism is the oldest religion in the world. It has three main branches of worship namely Saivisim, Vaishnavisim, and Sakhtism. It is more a way of life than rigid, common set of daily conducts. It has no single founder. It embraces numerous traditions and a wide range of moral, spiritual, and ethical codes of conduct for human life. Many seers and sages over thousands of years some say five thousand years back started contributing with their personal experiences by way of many Scriptures, Vedas, Upanishads, and Epics which have slowly become the main themes of Hinduism.

According to Dr. S.Radhakrishnan, "Hinduism is not a just faith. It is the union of reason and intuition that cannot be defined but is only to be experienced."

It lays emphasis on Paramathma or Brahma, the invisible power that creates, protects and dissolves. Humans are recognized as Jeevathmas. Jeevathmas can reach Paramathma's stage when they become spiritually elevated souls. Soul, self and athma, although recognized as one, are treated as equivalent to gods.

Four Maha Vakhyas—great sayings—as per Vedanta, are:

Prayanam Brahman—the supreme consciousness is Brahman, the creator.
Tat Tvam Asi—that thou art—That you are.
Ayam Atman Brahman—my consciousness is the creator.
Aham Brahmasmi—I am the creator
The main theme of Advaita in Hinduism is 'Sat-Chit-Ananda'—(existence, consciousness, peace).

Gayatri Mantra is highly revered mantra of Rigveda. It is in Sanskrit. The English transliteration is:

Om bhur Om bhuvah suvah
Tat Savitur Varenyam
Bhargo devasya dheemahi
Dhiyo yo nah prachodayat.

In the words of Swami Vivekananda, the English translation of Gayatri Mantra is as follows:

We meditate on the glory of that being who
has produced this universe;
May He enlighten our minds?

Similarly the omnipresent God's nature and worship is brought out in another Sanskrit poem:

"I bow to the supreme,
Who is not bound by the restraints of time and space?
Who is limitless consciousness?
Who was, is and ever will be who can be
realized only in oneself? Whose luminosity
knows no bounds; and who is an embodiment of peace,
I bow to the One, who pervades us all."

Bhartrihari
Sanskrit Poet
(Lived in 320 A.D to 544 AD)

Slowly, the concept of Brahma, Vishnu and Siva as the creator, protector and dissolver—the trinity, gained importance and remained as core aspect for worship by Hindus.

BUDDHISM

The teachings of Siddhartha Gautama became Buddhism when he was later called Buddha. He lived in India about 2500 years back. He attained enlightenment after deep meditation for a number of days under a Bodhi tree. He kept on teaching people till his last breadth about the ways of meeting the sufferings, attaining peace and happiness following the paths of ethical, devotional and meditative practices to attain liberation in life. Buddhism does not believe in worshipping a creator or personal God. It has two branches. One is called Mahayana ('The Great Vehicle") and the other Theravada ("The School of The Elders").

Buddhism emphasizes on Four Noble Truths and Eight Noble Paths as the core aspects of Buddhism.

Four Noble Truths are:

1) truth of suffering,
2) truth of the origin of suffering
3) truth of cessation of suffering
4) truth of the path to the cessation of suffering.

Eight Noble Paths are:

1) right understanding
2) right intention
3) right speech
4) right action
5) right livelihood
6) right effort
7) right mindfulness
8) right concentration

Buddham Sarnam Gacchami (I take refuge in Buddha)
Dharmam Sarnam Gacchami (I take refuge in Dharma)
Sangam Sarnam Gacchami (I take refuge in Sangha)

"It is better to conquer yourself
than to win a thousand battles.
Then the victory is yours.
It cannot be taken from you not by angels,
or by demons, Heaven or Hell."
"You are the source of all purity and impurity.
No one purifies another."

Buddha

CHRISTIANITY

Christianity comprises of mainly two branches; one is Protestants and the other is Catholics. It is the most popular religion in the world. It believes that there is one God, but there are three elements—trinity—to this one God: God the Father, God the Son, and The Holy Spirit.

The Holy Book of the Christianity is Bible. It consists of the Old and New Testaments. The core aspect of Christianity is the belief in Jesus Christ as the Son of God and the messiah (Christ). Jesus Christ is the visible manifestation of the invisible God. He was born in Circa 6 B.C in Bethlehem. He lived and preached and finally crucified. He is considered the incarnation of God. His teachings are examples of living a more spiritual life. Christians believe that he died for the sins of all people and rose from the dead.

"Your spiritual destiny is conditioned only by
your spiritual longings and purposes"

Urantia Book
156:5.9

"The Kingdom of God is within you."

Luke. 17:21

*"Know ye that ye are the temple of God and that the
spirit of God dewelleth in you."*

Corinthians 3:1

ISLAM

Islam is the second largest religion in the world. Mohammed (610-632) is the last prophet of God. He reported revelations that he believed to be form God and these teachings become Quran. Quran is the Holy Book regarded as the verbatim word of God. The follower of Islam is called Muslim. Muslims believe that God is one and incomparable. Allah is the name of the God the Almighty. He is the creator, sustainer, merciful and compassionate. Mohammed is his prophet.

According to Islam the purpose of existence is to submit and serve Allah. Religious concepts and practices include the Five Pillars of Islam. They are: 1) shahadah (creed), 2) daily prayers (salat), 3) almsgiving (Zakah), 4) fasting during Ramadan, 5) pilgrimage to Mecca (hajj). These are basic concepts and obligatory acts of worship. Following Islamic law which covers every aspect of life and society is essential part of Islam. It also provides guidance on multi various areas such as banking, welfare, warfare and environment.

There are mainly two sections of Muslims. They are: Sunni and Shia.

"Let's establish among ourselves and . . .
obey by heart the laws of Allah to lead a disciplined life
And let's pray for the prosperity of the whole world."

"Search for truth and you shall find beauty,
Search for beauty and you shall find love,
Search for love and you shall find God,
Search for God and you shall have them all."

Quran

JAINISM

The origins of Jainism are obscure. During the 5th century BCE, Vardhamana Mahāvīra became one of the most influential teachers of Jainism. Mahāvīra, however, was most probably not the founder of Jainism which reveres him as their prophet, not the author of their religion.

Jainism traditionally known as Jaina dharma is an Indian religion that prescribes a path of non-violence towards all living beings and emphasizes spiritual independence and equality between all forms of life. Practitioners believe that non-violence and self-control are the means by which they can obtain liberation. Currently, Jainism is divided into two major sects: digambara and svetambara.

The word Jainism is derived from a Sanskrit verb *Jin* which means *to conquer*. It refers to a battle with the passions and bodily pleasures that the *jaina* ascetics undertake. Those who win this battle are termed as *Jina* (conqueror). The term *Jaina* is therefore used to refer to laymen and ascetics of this tradition alike.

Jainism is one of the oldest religions in the world. Jains traditionally trace their history through a succession of twenty four propagators of their faith known as *tirthankara* with Ādinātha as the first *tirthankara* and Mahāvīra as the last of the current era.

> "He who looks inwardly at the self-reveals in the self;
> He who reveals in the self looks inwardly at the self.
> **Acaranga Sutra 2.173**

JUDAISM

Judaism is a monotheistic religion. The foundational text of Judaism is the Torah (Hebrew Bible). It is supported by the oral tradition represented by later texts such as the Mishnah and the Talmud. Judaism is considered by religious Jews to be the expression of the covenantal relationship God established with the the children of Israel.

Orthodox Judaism maintains that the Torah and Jewish law are divine in origin, eternal and unalterable, and that they should be strictly followed. It believes in one omniscient, omnipotent, benevolent and transcendent God. He created the universe and governs it.

> "Let the words of my mouth and the meditation of my heart be acceptable in thy sight O Lord, my rock and my redeemer."
>
> **Psalm**
> **(Judaism) 19.14**

> "Cast your burden on the Lord, and he will sustain you"
>
> **Psalm**
> (Judaism) 55.22.

SIKHISM

Sikhism is a monotheistic religion founded during the 16[th]century in the Punjab region of the Indian subcontinent by Guru Nanak The Guru Granth Sahib is a collection of the Sikh Guru's writings that was compiled by the 5th Sikh Guru. The followers of Sikhism are known as Sikhs.

Sikhism considers spiritual life and secular life to be intertwined. Guru Nanak, the first Sikh Guru established the system of the Langar, or communal kitchen, in order to demonstrate the need to share and have equality between all people. In addition to sharing with others Guru Nanak inspired people to earn an honest living without exploitation and also the need for remembrance of the divine name (God).

> "Contemplate solely the name of God . . .
> Fruitless are all other rituals."
>
> **Guru Granth Sahib**
> **Adi Granth su hi M.1**

SUFISM

Sufism is a religious branch historically derived from Sunni Islam. Some of the followers defined as the inner mystical dimension of Islam. Others contend that it is a perennial philosophy of existence that pre-dates religion, the expression of which flowered within Islam. Its essence has also been expressed via other religions and meta religious phenomena. A practitioner of this tradition is generally known as a Sufi.

Classical Sufi scholars have defined Sufism as "a science whose objective is the reparation of the heart and turning it away from all else but God."

It is above all creeds and all denominations and religions. It is a way of life—union with God.

"Everything you see has its roots in the unseen world. The forms may change, yet the essence remains the same.
Every wonderful sight will vanish; every sweet word will fade, but do not be disheartened,
The source they come from is eternal, growing, branching out, giving new life and new joy. Why do you weep?
The source is within you.

———◈———

Plunge, plunge into the vast ocean of consciousness,
Let the drop of water that is you become a hundred mighty seas, but do not think that the drop alone becomes the ocean, The Ocean too, becomes the drop."

Rumi

ZOROASTRIANISM

Zoroastrianism is an ancient Iranian religion and a religious philosophy. Zoroaster's ideas led to a formal religion bearing his name by about the 6th century BCE.

It believes in one God. The God is omnipresent, omnipotent and omniscient.

Besides all these religions, there are Confucianism, Taoism, Zen Buddhism and Shintoism. Slowly, over a period of some centuries, rituals were introduced and they have become more important than spiritual way of life. Many gods have come to stay as a means to achieve faith and belief. Codes of conduct were prescribed. Reward and punishment during lifetime and after death in the forms of Heaven and Hell were specified to ensure that humans observe the Codes of conduct. All religions similarly started following different kinds of rituals and religions have become an integral part of human life. Billions of people follow one religion or other and also they all adopt some or more rituals or other in life.

"I know more about religions now. Still, I am not able to understand spirituality. May I request you to elucidate more about it?"

"Sure. It is understandable. This is what His Holiness Dalai Lama once said:

> "It is more important to create safer,
> kinder world than to recruit more people to the
> religion that happens to satisfy us."

Spirituality and religion, although they relate closely to each other, there are differences between them. Basically, the spirituality means the quest for one's inner self and the divinity within each one of us. Religion, on the other hand, means a vast number of outward procedures, codes of conducts, moral and ethical ways, including prayers for worship and rituals.

> "Life is really about a spiritual unfolding
> that is personal and enchanting an
> unfolding that no science or philosophy
> or religion has yet fully clarified."
> **James Redfield**

Spirituality means something different from the perception of the senses. Intuitive power in everyone in addition to the body and mind which is the spirit plays a vital role in shaping the spirituality in humans.

The yearning of the soul is always different from the yearning of the body and mind. The soul is always looking out far beyond the ordinary horizon for deeper meaning and purpose. Outward objects and appearances have no relevance. It has inner self's aspirations for spiritual way of life with love, affection, compassion, empathy and above all love of God and love for every life in the world.

It is said 'inside out' and 'outside in'. This explains the way spirituality and religion operate.

> "You have to grow from the inside out.
> None can teach you, none can make you spiritual.
> There is no other teacher but your own soul."
> **Swami Vivekananda**

Similar views are echoed by many philosophers and thinkers.

> "Your vision will become clear only
> when you look into your heart.
> Who looks outside, dreams.
> Who looks inside, awakens."
> **Carl Jung**

"Thanks. I must say that I am now awakened. Is there any way for everyone to become spiritual?"

"Yes. The best way is to understand that everyone is fundamentally a spiritual being.

> "We are not human beings having a spiritual experience.
> We are spiritual beings having a human experience."
> **Teilhard de Chardin**

Continued spiritual practices enhance the purity of mind. When the mind becomes steady and still peace, quietness, harmony and positive achievements will come in one's way. Recent researches made by the neurosurgeons at the University of Pennsylvania proved that spiritual practices help to improve the physical and emotional health.

Some may feel that spirituality means that one should follow rigorous moral conduct by detaching and renouncing themselves from the normal way of life. But one, by living his own life, could still practice spirituality by his own understanding of the consciousness and live accordingly. Sogyal Rinpoche in his book,

'Tibetan Book of Living and Dying' explains that "True spirituality is to be aware that if we are interdependent, with everything and everyone else, even the smallest least significant thought, word, and action has real consequences throughout the universe."

To be spiritual, one should purify one's heart. Then one should follow one's heart. If that happens, spirituality can be realized in one's life. Spirituality is one among the other magical pathways to magical life. If one undertakes spiritual practices in everyday life then one can make one's life magical.

Regarding the aspect of how one can realize the spirituality in one's life, a story comes to my mind and the story is . . .

'After God created the universe, He decided to live in the midst of the humans. Every moment, the humans used to come and knock on His door and complain about everything. Why did you create a world full of problems? Why did you create bodies with sickness, old age and death? For what did you create sufferings for the humans? These were the questions they asked day and night. Sometimes they asked not to bring torrential rains, heaviest snows, hottest summers, and severest cold winter.

They kept on saying that either you bring extraordinarily more or severely less and create havocs and kill people. There were millions shouting and complaining that their prayers have not been answered. God did not have answers, but He got fed up with this kind of situation.

'He therefore summoned a group of angels and told them that millions of humans ask millions of questions every moment and He decided to dissolve Himself or take refuge in a place where the humans could not find Him.

One of the angels told God that He could move to Mount Everest, the highest peak in the Himalayas. God said that He is omniscient and He knows everything—past, present and future. Man has already set foot on Everest. They would build roads, houses, and bring airplanes, buses and all kinds of vehicles. They would find me and again I would be in the same old position. I might be forced again to move to another place.

'Another angel suggested that God might move to the moon. God said you do not know that man has already set foot on the moon also. They might start living on the moon and they would find me there. I would face the same old problems again. God asked, was there any other place he could move permanently?

'An old angel came forward and suggested that the only place the humans could never think of was within their own heart. God might go and sit there permanently.

'Thereafter, God disappeared from everywhere. Perhaps one could encounter something of divinity in one's own being. In one's life, one may find something that is godly.

One may also discover a quality, a fragrance, a presence, a certain air, a certain energy that belongs to the Universe and not to the human.'

Rabindranath Tagore

(Brief summary of one of his poems)

This will explain the nature of spirituality anyone can experience in one's life. The important aspects of these kinds of experiences lie in identifying, cultivating and nurturing not only for the benefit of one's own betterment of life but for the whole community. In this context I would like to mention what Arnold Toynbee wrote,

"The ultimate work of civilization is the unfolding of ever-deeper spiritual understanding."

Daisaku Ikeda echoed the same view which is very relevant in this context: "How aware are we of our own inner life, our spirituality—something so intangible yet so priceless? How much effort do we make to perceive that which is not obvious, which can neither be seen nor heard? I believe the exploration and enrichment of the human spirit is what determines our very humanity. Such enrichment provides an inner compass that can lead civilizations to greatness."

"Thanks for the excellent story. I am extremely thankful to you. If you permit, may I take leave of you?"

"Yes; of course. When we meet again, we may discuss whether the happiness is a mirage or real. You may, therefore, apply your mind and come with your findings. Good day," the old one told the young one and both took leave of each other.

CHAPTER 6

Happiness

Happiness is when what you think, what you say and what
you do are in harmony.

Mahatma Gandhi

"**G**ood Morning. I am very happy to meet you today. For a very long time I did not see you. Last time I met you, you asked me to apply my mind on 'is happiness a mirage or real?' and meet you with my findings.' I did attempt to understand what happiness is. As usual I am clouded with confusion. I think happiness is not a mirage; it is real and everyone wants to be happy. Please help me to understand correctly." The young one told the old one".

"How do you say that happiness is not mirage? First, we should try to understand what happiness is.

"Every man wants to be happy but in order to be so; he
needs first to understand what happiness is."

Jean Jacques Rousseau

Happiness is generally understood as 'giving or causing pleasure.' Happiness, pleasure, and joy are the words usually used to express the feeling or state of mind. What you say may be the general belief of the people. Daisaku Ikeda said that "What is the purpose of life? It is to become happy. Whatever country or society people live in they all have the same deep desire to become happy."

"Yes. If one gets money, power, fame, relationship, wealth, robust health, success or popularity or one or two of such things, then he is happy. People will always relate happiness to enjoyment of money or power or fame or relationship, or robust health or popularity. Those who do not have them, *try very hard to get them. If they do not get them, then they will feel unhappy. This happens to everyone in life. Is it not true?"*

"What you say may be the general belief of the people. But the truth is,

"Those who seek happiness in pleasure, wealth, glory, power and heroics are as naive as the child who tries to catch a rainbow and wear it as a coat"
Dilgo Khyentse Rinpoche

Irrespective of whatever one possesses, one always looks out for something else with the result that everyone lives a life of unfulfilled wants and desires. Humans are always in search of happiness. The search goes on and on even when one gets what one wants to get in life. Sometimes the search appears to be endless. The satisfaction levels seem to have no limit in itself. This is what Socrates once said that "If you don't get what you want, you suffer; if you get what you don't want, you suffer; even when you get exactly what you want, you still suffer because you can't hold on to it forever. Your mind is your predicament."

A story explains this phenomenon very clearly:

'There was a king who one day posed a question in his court. He promised to give anything in his kingdom who answered his question correctly. The question was, "was there anything in the world which would satisfy a desire of a human?" Everyone in the court from his ministers onwards tried their best to answer the question. Someone said money. Other one said power. Many said wealth. One of them said popularity, robust health and so on. But none of the answers satisfied the king.

When the court was to be adjourned, suddenly a man with a long beard and a bowl looked like a beggar appeared and said that he would answer the question. The man requested the king whether he could arrange to have his little bowl filled with some food. The king ordered to fill the bowl. The bowl was filled with the food but the next moment the food vanished.

The man kept on asking the king to fill the bowl till it got filled. But whatever was placed into the bowl was vanishing. The king was astonished. He kept on placing everything he had. The bowl like a bottomless pit was empty all the time as everything placed into it was vanishing every time.

The king did not know what was happening and felt totally annoyed. He with his annoyance asked the strange man what he was doing with his bowl and whether he was playing magic in his court. Finally the man explained to the bewildered king that the secret was that the bowl was made up of human mind and desires.'

This shows that the wants and desires of humans never get satisfied. According to Cicero, "The thirst for desire is never filled, nor fully satisfied."

> "We seek pleasures in the pursuit of various desires and objects and still remain dissatisfied."
>
> **Anonymous**

To put it in a more clear perspective, according to a Tibetan saying, "Seeking happiness outside ourselves is like waiting for sunshine in a cave facing north."

This is the reality. Happiness is the evasive illusion of the mind. If one makes it a habit of pursuing happiness in everything one does and in everything one plans to achieve, then happiness will become elusive and unhappiness will become certain. The truth therefore lies elsewhere. Descartes was emphatic when he said, "I have made it my habit to alter my desires rather than the order of the world."

Happiness always presupposes unhappiness. How many of those who have everything in life such as money, health, wealth, power, popularity, and success are truly happy? Democritus was clear when he said that "Happiness resides not in possessions and not in gold; happiness dwells in the soul." The richest people always say that something is missing in their life. The people who enjoy unlimited power always live their lives on knives' edge. The people who have unlimited popularity and fame live in cocoons.

Every one of such people feels unsecured and openly admits that something is missing in their life. Helen Keller echoed the same sentiment when she said, "Happiness cannot come from without. It must come from within."

Humans always make happiness as the only purpose of living and sacrifice everything including their physical and mental health to acquire and possess anything and everything to satisfy their urge for happiness. The heart, the soul, the spirit, the virtues, and the values are all sacrificed at the altar of the elusive happiness.

Dr. Denis Waitley therefore said "Happiness cannot be traveled to, owned, earned, worn, or consumed. Happiness is the spiritual experience of living every minute with love, grace and gratitude." Aurobindo wrote that "You may possess things but you must not be possessed by them."

Humans work to earn money for livelihood. Mahatma Gandhi said "There is enough in the world to meet everyone's need and not the greed." If this is realized, then there is no problem either to the individual or to the society. But when the humans become possessed by the greed then no amount of money or wealth will ever satisfy them.

> "Money never made a man happy yet, nor will it.
> There is nothing in its nature to produce happiness.
> The more a man has, the more he wants.
> Instead of filling a vacuum, it makes one."
>
> **Bible**

Money and wealth alone will never bring happiness. Whenever humans chase money and wealth they mostly sacrifice their health or health becomes the first victim of the mirage chase. Many times when the lost health becomes irreversible the humans blink without having the health to enjoy the money and wealth.

Similarly success will never give enduring happiness. Success will always push humans from one success to another and the pushing will go on endlessly. On the other hand, happiness will lead to success.

"Success is not the key to happiness.
Happiness is the key to success."
Albert Schweitzer

I hope all the wisdom sayings will help you to catch up with me."

"I am getting more confused as usual. You are always looking at things in a very different way from others. You say the truth lies elsewhere. Where the truth lies?"

"Do not be impatient. The truth is not visible as lies. Similarly happiness is not visible as unhappiness. People believe that happiness lies outside of them. They think that acquiring wealth, accumulating material objects, securing relationships and falling into addictions etc. will bring happiness.

This shows that happiness depends on certain conditions to be fulfilled. In other words, conditionality is always knowingly or unknowingly attached to happiness. If you look at closely, such things do bring some happiness which is called ego satisfaction of the false-self. (Ego is one of the faces of the false—self). Such happiness is momentary and not stable and lasting. Such happiness vanishes as soon as the condition is fulfilled.

"Our greatest happiness does not depend on the condition
of life in which chance has placed us, but is always the
result of a good conscience, good health, occupation, and
freedom in all just pursuits."
Thomas Jefferson

"You as usual are adding more confusion to my already confused mind. Could you not explain it in a simple and brief way?"

"My friend, I always try to be brief and clear. But your impatience over takes your listening. However, I try to complete it as quickly as possible. I said people believe that happiness lies outside of them. Truly happiness lies inside of them. This means that no conditionality is attached to true happiness. Happiness is therefore inside job."

"If it is inside job, why people are always in search of happiness elsewhere?"

"It is a good question. It is because that human mind acts like a monkey. As monkey jumps from one branch to another branch of a tree, human mind constantly jumps from one desire to another to find happiness. The restlessness, higher level of expectations, and insatiable nature of human mind manifests itself in searching happiness everywhere and every time endlessly. The result is unhappiness. This unhappiness pushes everyone to search new avenues of happiness which becomes a mirage."

Swami Rama once said that, "What good does it do to have all the riches of the world and all the world's pleasures? They will all disappear in the flash we call a human lifetime. Focusing on the pleasures of the world keeps the mind too distracted to search for the inner self." According to Albert Einstein, "A life directed chiefly towards the fulfillment of personal desires sooner or later always leads to bitter disappointment,"

"I am sorry to interrupt. You mean to say that a large number of people in the world including the rich countries are unhappy in their lives?"

Happy Planet Index (HPI) of 2012 after studying and rating 151 countries in the world says that nine out of top ten happiest countries in the world are located in the Caribbean Basin, despite high levels of poverty. Among the top five world's biggest economies in terms of GDP, Japan ranks way down in 45thplace, Germany 46th, France 50th, China 60th, and the USA 105th, due to their environmental footprint of 7.5, the highest among the 151 countries studied. HPI is an index of human well-being, life expectancy levels, and environmental impact. This is totally different from Gross Domestic Product (GDP) index and Human Development Index (HDI). (Wikipedia).This clearly shows that there is no direct correlation between the richness and happiness.

Similarly, one will have to relate the levels of depression to the levels of happiness. The more the levels of depression, the more the unhappiness people experience in their lives.

A study was sponsored by the World Health Organization, in 2011, by interviewing more than eighty nine thousand people in eighteen different countries.

According to the study, the prevalence of major depressive episodes in those eighteen countries is France 21%, USA 19.2%, Brazil 18.4% Netherlands 17.9%, New Zealand 17.8%, Ukraine 14.6%, Belgium 14.1%, Colombia 13.3%, Lebanon 10.9%, Spain 10.6%, Israel 10.2%, Italy 9.9%, Germany 9.9%, South Africa 9.8%, India 9%, Mexico 8%, Japan 6.6%, and China 6.5%.

On average, 15 per cent of people in high-income countries reported having an episode, compared with 11 per cent in low-income countries, according to the study, published in July 25 2011 in the journal BMC Medicine.

Depression affects nearly 121 million people worldwide and is the second leading contributor to shorter lifespan and poor health for individuals 15-44 years of age, according to the Geneva based WHO.

The higher percentage of depression reported by people in wealthier countries may reflect differences in societal expectations for a good life. Ronald Kessler the co-author of the study said, "There are a lot of people in the U.S. who say they aren't satisfied with their lives," Kessler, a professor of health care policy at Harvard Medical School, in Boston, Massachusetts, further said in an interview that "In U.S. expectations know no bounds and people in other countries are just happy to have a meal on the table."

Mihaly Csikszentmihalyi a leading scholar in the field of positive psychology, once asked a very simple question, "If we are so rich why aren't we happy."

As I mentioned earlier happiness does not depend on outward conditions. Hugh Downs says that "A happy person is not a person in a certain set of circumstances, but rather a person with a certain set of attitudes." Truly the state of mind and attitude decide the level of happiness. No other outward objects, circumstances, incidents, possessions, and wealth will ever provide enduring happiness.

In reality what Dan Millman said is true: "There is no path to happiness; happiness is the path." Mihaly Csikszentmihalyi, in his book, 'The Psychology of Optimal Experience' says that "People who learn to control inner experience will be able to determine the quality of their lives, which is as close as any of us can come to being happy."

"You have gone somewhere without answering my question. Please come back and help me to understand correctly."

"You interrupted me in the middle of our discussion. Anyway, I will now explain about inside job to find happiness. Maha Upanishad talks about 4 doors of salvation which according to me applies equally to happiness. They are:

- Sham (restraint)
- Vichar (thinking and contemplation)
- Santosh (Contentment)
- Satsang (good company)

In this context I will tell you what Rumi, the greatest Sufi philosopher once wrote: "I have lived in the lip of insanity wanting to know reasons, knocking on the door. The door opens. I have been knocking from the inside."

People are looking out for happiness outside of them as they search for God outside of them. If the mind is trained to look inside for love, peace, self-restraint, appreciation, harmony and contentment, then happiness will follow automatically. One should find the true self and try to cultivate the way of listening to the inner self. The inner self always open the door for happiness. The heart is the seat where lies the true driving force of happiness. In the words of Daisaku Ikeda "What is true victory in life? What is the meaning of true happiness? Who is truly great? The answer to such questions is determined not by superficial criteria such as fame, status and wealth, but by the inner reality of one's heart".

> "My crown is in my heart not on my head.
> Not decked with diamonds and Indian stones,
> Nor to be seen; my crown is called Content,
> A crown it is that seldom kings enjoy."
>
> **Shakespeare—Henry VI**

In fact Socrates wrote with contempt that "Contentment is natural wealth, luxury is artificial poverty." I am sure that at least now you may understand what I am trying to explain."

"Sorry. I am slow in understanding. Please say it again".

"My friend I will tell you in a different way. Tao says, "I have three treasures which I hold fast and watch closely. The first is compassion; the second is moderation, the third is humility." Tao also says, "Contentment alone is enough. Indeed, the bliss of eternity can be found in your contentment."

"You mean to say that happiness is a mind's game."

"You may say so. The fact is that the desires rise in the mind like waves in the ocean in every split second. That is why, Blair Lewis warns that, "Protect your mind at all costs. Clean your mind at every opportunity. Do not harbor unwanted and unneeded guest in your mind."

He concludes, "In order to feel worthy of true internal happiness, you need to accept yourself, your personality and your personal history. Happiness is an innermost core of your being and is therefore available to you regardless of your past. Since happiness is already within you, you need only to create conditions in your life and body that enable you to feel its presence."

"I am happy that I could understand now what one should do to find happiness. Is there anything more which I should understand to feel happier in my life?"

"Yes. Tal Ben-Shahar wrote that, "Happiness is not about making it to the peak of the mountain nor is it about climbing aimlessly around the mountain. Happiness is the experience of climbing toward the peak."

One day in the early morning hours I was sitting in a bench in one corner of a park after taking my usual walk. A fat, wealthy gentleman came and sat near me. He introduced himself saying that he was Roy. He was a billionaire having four children and three grand children. He built an empire of industries and businesses.

At the age of fifty he was diagnosed of having heart problems. He had repeated treatments one after the other leading finally to replacement of heart. He said he was not afraid of death but wanted to live his life in happiness and peace. He also said that lately he discovered that he had never been happy in his life and looking back he wasted his life. Having realized he now wanted to find happiness in his life. In his search for happiness he wasted his fortune in exotic holidays, extravagant health resorts, adventurous mountaineering, trekking holidays, cruise's tours and visiting every other country in the world map. But nothing satisfied him and the happiness was still elusive. The only thing he found was his health had deteriorated threatening his life. He asked me was there any other way to find happiness.

I was shocked to hear his story. However I told him that he was looking all the time outside for happiness. Instead, looking inside would help even at this time of his life. Perhaps his insatiable nature added with unlimited wealth would have caused his problems. The pathways of simplicity in the midst of wealth, humility, yoga and meditation, love, compassion, and service would help him. I explained to him in detail about these pathways. His face got brightened. He took leave of me with thanks that he would follow these pathways and come back to me with happiness.

Everyone as in the case of Roy is always in search of happiness. But happiness is elusive as mirage. But to achieve enduring happiness in one's life one will have to look inside and understand the inner self. This can be easily achieved by training the mind to become calm and quiet. Yoga and meditation will help to train the mind.

In the eloquence of the silence and quietness of the mind with focus and mindfulness one can still the mind. In this state of consciousness the inner self reveals itself and one can identify, cultivate and nurture so that one can hear the inner voice. When the mind is achieved this state of higher level of consciousness then one can train the mind to change the attitudes.

This can be achieved by regular interactions with the self. The attitudes of love, compassion, appreciation, gratitude, kindness, realizations, contentment, will lead one to understand the purpose, and meaning of life. All these will have to be internalized. These are the magical pathways which will provide all the ingredients for this purpose. The magical pathways will certainly help everyone to achieve a state of enduring happiness in one's life.

His Holiness Dalai Lama said that "As human beings we all want to be happy and free from misery... we have learned that the key to happiness is inner peace. The greatest obstacles to inner peace are disturbing emotions such as anger, attachment, fear and suspicion, while love and compassion and a sense of universal responsibility are the sources of peace and happiness." Also I would like to say that according to Sir Laurens van der post,

"There is nothing wrong in searching for happiness.
But of far more comfort to the soul . . . .
Is something greater than happiness or
unhappiness?
and that is meaning.
because meaning transfigures all . . . .
Once what you are doing has for you meaning
it is irrelevant whether you are happy or unhappy.
You are content—you are not alone
In your spirit—you belong."

Before I conclude another old story which had been in circulation for a very long time comes to my mind. The story goes:

'An Australian billionaire went on a fishing holiday to a Fiji island. One day he sat near local Fijian who was fishing in the coast. The Australian tried again and again but he could not catch a single fish. The Fijian caught 3 fishes in quick succession and started leaving the place.

The Australian in his astonishment asked the Fijian 'Why are you leaving, when you can catch more fishes?' This question led to an interesting conversation between them which went along the following lines:

'Sir, this satisfies my need. I live with my wife and son. My wife will cook and we take one fish for each of us and enjoy ourselves.' The Fijian replied.

'If you catch more, you can sell and get money.' Australian said.

'Then, what happens?'

'If you get money you can employ people to catch fishes and sell and get more money.'

'Then what happens?'

'When you get more money you can buy a trawler and catch more fishes and sell more. You will earn more money.'

'Then, what happens?'

'You can multiply your catches by increasing the trawlers and employing more people. By this you will multiply your money Slowly you can become a millionaire. When you multiply further you can export and one day you will become a billionaire like me.'

'How long will it take?'

'It might take say ten to fifteen years. Then you can go on a fishing holiday to find happiness and enjoy yourself.'

'Why should I do all those things for so many years and finally go for fishing to find happiness? I am already doing it and enjoying myself.' Fijian closed the discussion and went home."

"This story explains in nutshell what you have been telling me so far. This is a very interesting story. I am blessed to be here with you to—day. I do not know how to thank you. Please accept my hearty thanks."

"I should on the other hand, thank you for meeting me to-day. We need not thank each other. It is a dialogue you and me are having on our journey of finding the truths of life. Before you meet me next time, please collect your thoughts on 'Choices and Balance' and we try to put our thoughts together and find out the truth. Good day".

CHAPTER 7

Choices And Balance

"Your life is the sum result of all the choices you make,
both consciously and unconsciously.
If you can control the process of choosing, you can take
control of all aspects of your life.
You can find the freedom that comes from being in the
charge of yourself."

Robert F. Bennett

"The best and safest thing is to keep a balance in your life,
acknowledge the great powers around us and in us. If you
can do that, and live that way, you are really a wise man."

Euripides
(484 B.C—406 B.C)

"*G*ood morning. Last time we met, you asked me to reflect on 'the choices and the balance'. I did reflect and felt that there is nothing that one could do about the choices and the balance. The way one lives today, in these modern times, whatever comes one's way, one will have to take it and go on with the life. Is it not true?" the young one asked the old one.

"It looks as if you have not reflected on this matter seriously. Do you think that there are no problems in making choices that are available and the necessity to adopt a balance in day-to-day life? Why one would have to choose and balance? This is mainly because one will have to fulfill one's needs and desires. Needs and desires not only multiply but also keep changing like waves in the ocean. To match these with the multiplicity of choices which are also increasing day by day creates problems in choosing and balancing."

"There may be problems and also difficulties. But these are there for everyone. How to face and resolve these problems is a major obstacle. The people, therefore, choose whatever they can and go on with the life. Is there any other way to deal with them?"

"I am glad that you have now come to understand that there are problems. These choices were not many in earlier days. There were only a few or no choices at all. People also were not aware of the choices and many a time they were not made easily available to them. Life, therefore, was very simple. But today, due to the development in science and technology and the speed of the transportation, the choices have multiplied to an extraordinary level. In addition, multitasking by every human is also multiplying day by day. Therefore, they have also brought problems of balance along with their emergence.

> "We cannot lead a choice less life.
> Every day, every moment, every second, there is a choice.
> If it were not so, we would not be individuals."
> **Ernest Holmes**

"Now I understand. Sorry for my simplistic way of looking at matters. Do you mean that choices are not good and they affect the people?"

"Choices are good. Nature provides varieties of choices. Perhaps humans are impacted by the nature in this respect as well. When the choices are many, to choose one among many becomes difficult. Some call it tyranny of choices. The more the choices one has, the more one gets confused. You take any aspect of human life today, whether it relates to the babies', school children's, adult's, middle, and old-age people's needs and wants, there are thousands of choices available regarding their food, dress, education, jobs, entertainments, holidays, finances, homes, transports, travels, celebrations, medicines and relationships. The question is how to make the correct choice and at the same time how to see that the balance is maintained."

"I don't still think that there is a serious problem. You seem to imagine that everyone is suffering. To my mind, these problems are imaginary and superficial."

"Maybe; if you look at them superficially, they may look as if they are not real and important in life. But they are very real. I will tell you one by one for your benefit, although they are very elementary in their nature. Take food, there are thousands of varieties and brands available, whether for babies or for adults. Every day, a new product or food is being introduced and marketed. The same way, the dress poses problems of ever-changing fashions and ever increasing varieties of items. Similarly, the educational field offers numerous courses in hitherto unknown areas.

Varieties of jobs and new awareness of opportunities are being made available everywhere. Varieties of the core aspects of the entertainment industry, which uses effectively the modern techniques and offers lifelines to the people's living. Any number of holiday packages is being made available with the attractive offers. New, innovative products for savings and investments are being introduced every day. Homes of various designs, facilities and fitted with modern accessories are available now.

Similarly, every day, newly designed bicycles, cars, buses and planes with improved technology for comfort, safety and speed are being introduced. Travel with ever-changing facilities has become part of everyday existence. Celebrations have introduced varieties of methods and facilities. Medicines and hospitals are also following the varieties routes. Varieties are the spices of life. As far as the relationships are concerned, they have taken different routes and ways of living, either together or away from each other, but still finding a way to live a life of married or not married existence."

"Why have all these developments happened, besides the development in science and technology?"

"Developments in science and technology have improved and impacted every aspect of human life in modern times. When such improvements, innovations, discoveries, and developments have occurred, they are patented and branded by the multi-billion dollar commercial establishments to sell them on a commercial basis all over the world. They use print, electronic and other media with modern techniques of photography and music to visually and mentally impact the minds and the hearts of the people. The producers keep introducing different kinds of products of the same quality in different names and with new packaging at different times.

Humanity at least in this aspect is united in adopting mostly the same kind of food, dress, drinks, vehicles, houses, other household articles and relationships with day to day changes. Within this uniformity of development there lie varieties of choices one will have to make in everyday life. People are, therefore, getting confused to make correct choices at the correct time."

"Is it because the materialism, as you used to say, along with the commercialization and globalization, has contributed more to this problem of choices?"

"You are right. The problem of choices is mainly due to the fact that no one likes to understand that there is a problem. Even if anyone understands the problem, the following contributory factors' influence the minds of humans more powerfully than any understanding. The result is that most of the time humans are making wrong choices and facing unhappiness and misery. Take for example instead of choosing sweet words humans sometimes choose to use harsh, offensive and provocative words. Similarly instead of doing good deeds sometimes humans choose to do bad deeds. All these arise only because of one's bad thoughts and bad choices.

> "I believe that we are solely responsible for our choices, and we have to accept the consequences of every deed, word, and thought throughout our lifetime."
> **Elizabeth Kubler-Ross**

The contributory factors which I mentioned earlier are:

1) The availability of multiple choices,
2) Attractive packaging to catch the eyes and the mind,
3) Inducements by effective, seductive, and penetrative advertisements,
4) Repeated print, electronic, radio and TV advertisements to impact one's mind and heart,

5) Affordability of people by effectively using the economies of large-scale production, distribution and selling outlets,
6) Bringing and increasing multiplicity of products,
7) Branding and maintaining brands,
8) Online selling and buying,
9) Easily accessible money through multiple credit cards system,
10) Hectic way of life leaving no time to think and choose,

This does not mean that all these developments are bad. They are good. They have come to stay whether one likes them or not. They will keep on increasing in future as well. These are evolutionary process. No one can either stop or get away from them. But the question is how one should face the reality and make correct choices and make one's life worth living.

"Are there any other factors other than those you have already mentioned?"

"Yes, of course. What we have seen are only the external factors. There are also internal factors. They are:

(a) awareness and knowledge,
(b) the needs, the wants and the desires,
(c) the impulsiveness,
(d) the insatiable wants and desires,
(e) the greed,
(f) comparing with others,
(g) vulnerability of human mind,
(h) time constraint,

"May I request you to elaborate on all these internal factors?"

"These internal factors will impact every human, one way or other, either mildly or severely whenever one will to have to make a choice consciously or unconsciously.

Once the choice is made the consequences of such choice whether good or bad will have to be faced. In some cases the consequences may be of short term nature. But in many cases they may change the entire course of one's life with long term impact. It all depends on the nature of the matter on which one makes a choice.

"We choose our joys and sorrows long before them."

Kahlil Gibran

AWARENESS AND KNOWLEDGE

One should cultivate the awareness of one's own environment. One should develop the knowledge of the various products, services, locations, qualities, of the material objects before making any choice. Similarly every other aspects of human life are concerned one should always cultivate the awareness and knowledge of such aspects of life. Also one should keep the awareness whether they are suitable for the environment, health and purpose. They should also conform to the local laws, family values and community values.

Some long term matters such as education, job, house, marriage, children, health, and old age etc. require a lot of studies, thinking and analyzing before any decision is made on such matters. Hasty decisions will have severe impact and the consequences will affect the very peaceful existence of life itself.

THE NEEDS, THE WANTS AND THE DESIRES

Needs are far more important than the wants and the desires. Even then one should evaluate one's needs and prioritize them. The wants and desires will always multiply. Checking and re-checking will possibly reduce the numbers and mostly help to make needed and correct choices.

Buying for the sake of buying will add only to the clutter and serve no purpose. Availability of money easily either own or on credits will unconsciously induce the mind to multiply the unnecessary wants and desires. In addition unwanted needs also get added day by day. Only caution and awareness of what is necessary alone will help any human being.

THE IMPULSIVENESS

The impulsive nature will always result in wastages, loss of money, time and energy. Once the impulsive nature of making choices becomes a habit then it will only add misery and unhappiness. Those who indulged in impulsiveness in their childhood develop slowly the habit of choosing and doing everything on the basis of impulsiveness. Unless this aspect is corrected this habit will always lead to a lot of avoidable problems in life.

THE INSATIABLE WANTS AND DESIRES

The insatiable nature is dangerous to the body, the mind, the spirit, the money and life. Insatiable nature develops mostly in the minds of the humans when they fall into the habit of thinking, speaking, and doing the things which cannot fit in with the time, age, period, culture and environment.

There is time for everything; time to study, play, eat, and sleep. There is age for everything; age for study, marriage, work, retirement, and rest. There is period for everything; period (time for completion) for study, understanding, maturity and practice. There is culture in everything; culture in family, community, society, workplace, state and nation. There is environment; environment in dwelling (place), playing, working, traveling, living-village, town, city-state, nation and world. Humans when ignore these basic factors and interchange everything and indulge in overdoing then they develop insatiable nature which can never be fulfilled in anyone's life time.

Cultivating the nature of contentment, fulfillment and satisfaction is only the cure.

THE GREED

Greed shuts the doors of one's intelligence, knowledge, values, power, slowly and subtly and makes one totally blind even to the laws, the environment, health, family and even the self existence. Greed is self-destructive in nature.

The self pride, unrealistic ego, insatiable desires, wants, needs, lead one to take the path of greed in a blindfolded way and finally destroy what has been achieved and created all through one's life with struggle and many sacrifices.

COMPARING WITH OTHERS

One will have to live the life of one's own and not the life of others. Comparing all the time with what the neighbors, the relatives, the friends and others have and trying to match with their possessions and behaviors will always result in chaos. To eliminate this aspect is the only way to happiness.

There are three types of people who live their lives as per their own choices they consciously choose to follow in their life:

1. The one who lives his/her life as his/her own and not of anybody's life;
2. The one who lives to satisfy the perception of others;
3. The one who lives in comparing his life to the lives of others.

While the second and third categories of people live their life as other's life and their life for others will always find their life as painful, the first category of people will always find life as magical.

VULNERABILITY OF HUMAN MIND

The mind is always vulnerable. It will easily be influenced by the powerful unwanted desires and wants. To be aware of the vulnerability and take precaution not to fall prey will have to be cultivated and practiced.

TIME CONSTRAINT

Time is not the constraint. When one is always kept on the run and rush, one cannot find time to make choices. Time must be found to understand and analyses to make correct choices.

Dannion Brinkley in his book,' Secrets of the Light' says that, "Life is a matter of choice. Everything we manifest in our day to day lives is the direct result of our choices along the way. Each choice automatically creates a consequence. From our choices other people's lives are influenced for better or worse. Therefore our choices need to be made carefully. Every single thing that one of us thinks says or does, impacts all the rest of humanity on one level or another".

To sum up I would like to say:

a) Some people make wrong choices and suffer, wondering why others live happily
b) Some people make wrong choices and correct in the mid—course and reach the destination halfway.
c) Some people never choose and leave to others and the time to make the choices and float around in the midstream of the river of their life.
d) Some people make correct choices at the correct time and lead a life of fulfillment."

The other day I was having my snack and coffee in a famous local club. I had lot friends in that club. That day at least five of them met me and shared their experiences in life when the subject of choices in life came up for discussion. One after the other shared their experiences with the present day situation in their life.

Robinson shared his secret of how he took a decision in haste and impulsiveness to become an engineer against his parents' wishes and still suffer with pain why he had chosen that profession in which he could not put his heart and soul and succeed.

John said that mistaking infatuation as love he went ahead with his marriage at the very early age which ended up in divorce after two years with lot of pain. This incident still haunts him and prevents him from making a choice in favor of marriage.

Nancy shared how she made a good choice of going for business management course in Harvard Business School which helped her to become a CEO of a global business conglomerate.

Ram confessed that he was his parent's parrot and made his parents to make choices for him. This abdication of his responsibility for the sake of his own convenience or want of time made him suffer in his marriage, job, and raising children.

Karan joined the group late but he made his point very clear that every one without parental guidance and personal knowledge made wrong choices in early age and later part of life as well. He made a wrong choice of working for a big company away from home, against his wife's wish, with no connection to his qualification but only for big money.

With fat money coming in he committed for big mortgages for two huge houses, three big cars, heavy insurance, and three children's elite education. He suffered at the hands of unscrupulous seniors and ruthless C.E.O for ten years. He had to put up with this kind of suffering only because of heavy mortgages. In fact he mortgaged his life itself for money and not able to get out of the trap and he suffered silently for years. Due to this suppressed suffering for a long time he suffered a heart attack in the early age of his life. He survived with great difficulty and decided to quit. He later joined a medium sized company for a lesser salary, closer to his home and revived his existence with care and happiness.

"Thank you for helping me to understand the contemporary problem. I am now clear about making the correct choices. May I now request you to tell me about the balance in life?"

"Life itself is a balancing act. Balance in life is like a rope walking in a circus. Everyone will look at the circus artist with awe when he walks with a long pole on his hands to balance on the rope tied between two stands with a distance of about twenty feet and with a height of about ten feet above the ground. This is a metaphor of everyone's life, how one will have to balance and lead a successful life.

It means that one will have to balance between one's body and the mind, the money and the time, the family life and the working life, personal life and social life, and the friendships and the relationships. If anyone of these aspects is given more attention than the other in the pair then latter one will suffer and bring in enormous problems. These problems slowly and decisively manifest in the form of worry, anxiety, anger, jealousy, stress, strain and finally ill health, and unhappiness. "

"I know life is a struggle for millions of people. What has balance to do with this phenomenon?"

"To face the struggle and come out of its influence on life, one will have to understand the nature and the real benefit of balance in one's life. As one faces dualities in everything that exists, one will have to basically be aware of this nature's creative intelligence and the purpose. Nature has created female and male in every species on the planet for the purpose of procreation. Women and men are created in humans.

Each one has some features of the other. In Hinduism, the concept of the God, 'Arthanaareeshwarar', half of woman and the other half of man in one form from head to toe, is being worshiped to highlight this fact.

The present-day psychologists say that each woman and man has some features of the other in each one of them. In China, the concept is being celebrated in the form of Yin and Yang.

The scientists say that left side of the body is wired to the right side of our brain and the right side of the body to left side of the brain. Similarly, in human brain there are two parts: left hemisphere and right hemisphere.

The characteristics of the left hemisphere are different from the characteristics of the right hemisphere."

The left side brain's characteristics are:

- uses logic;
- detail oriented;
- facts rule;
- words and languages;
- present and past;
- comprehending;
- knowing;
- reality based;

- practical;
- safe.

The right side brain's characteristics are:

- uses feelings;
- imagination;
- symbols and images;
- present and future;
- philosophy and religion;
- meaning;
- believing;
- appreciating;
- spatial perception;
- fantasy based;
- presents possibilities;
- risk taking.

This kind of imbalance creates the present-day problems in human life. Again, if you take the body, we have two eyes, two ears, two hands and two legs. Nature's creation in itself warrants balance between these organs or limbs of the body."

"It looks as if I am getting into an unknown area of science. Is it all necessary for a person of my generation to waste time on such matters?"

"It all depends on how one desire to lead a successful and fulfilling life with meaning. For this purpose, knowledge and awareness are as necessary as your food, air, water, and drinks."

"I got it. Please proceed."

"The other area that requires balance is intelligence. Humans are provided with intellect that appears to be infinite in nature. The best brains, including that of Albert Einstein, have reportedly used only up to 5% of their power of the brain.

By evolution, each generation is adding more and more intelligence because the base to start from has been widened and advanced.

In the beginning of the 20th century, IQ—Intelligence Quotient—has assumed a lot of attention. Psychologists introduced various tests for measuring it. These tests measured the intelligence of the people. The higher the IQ, it was said the higher the intelligence. This theory was practiced for quite some time to sort out humans on the basis of these tests. But, later on it was found out that I.Q alone is not enough and there are other hidden intelligences which are also important to measure the power of human intellect.

> "The winner's edge is not in a gifted birth, a high I.Q, or in talent. The winner's edge is all in the attitude, not aptitude. Attitude is the criterion for success."
>
> **Denis Waitley**

"In the year 1994, Daniel Goleman, with the aid of various researches done by neuroscientists and psychologists, brought out a theory known as Emotional Intelligence, EQ—Emotional Quotient—which acquired equal or more importance. It gives humans compassion, motivation and empathy. It has to be learned, cultivated, and nurtured. It is Plato who said that "All learning has an emotional base."

"At the end of the 20th century, research done further brought out another area of intelligence, which is now called Spiritual Intelligence S.Q—Spiritual Quotient. SQ is considered to measure the spiritual aspect of one's intelligence like the EQ is considered to measure the cognitive intelligence. SQ is concerned with the self-awareness, higher level of consciousness, inner self, the purpose and meaning of life. It makes humans different from other animals or artificial intelligence of computers and other machines. It is not concerned about any religion or any sect. But it is the inner self of the body which moves the mind towards higher consciousness and tries to provide values for human actions and meaning for the purpose of life.

It is now realized that the SQ is necessary for the effective functioning of both IQ and EQ. These three basic intelligences are to be in harmony with each other and, for that purpose, proper balance of attitude has become absolutely necessary in the fast changing human life.

Recently another theory which has come to occupy the central stage in this context is Social Intelligence. It is said that man is a social animal. Also, the man is not an island. Any human is not only interconnected but also interacts continuously with other humans and with the community and society as well. It is the ability to get along well with others and get them to cooperate with one another.

"Thank you; may I ask you how an ordinary human can use balance for his purposeful living?"

"One will have to understand the nature's choices, which are made available through the body, the mind and the spirit. Without choices there is no life to live. Choices are essence of life. Making a choice requires a lot of knowledge, patience, and vision on life. Then, starting from the balanced food for the body, balanced way of using our own organs and limbs, one can maintain equilibrium in our bodily existence. As far as the mind is concerned, balancing our emotions, feelings, intelligence, thoughts, and attitudes will make one steady and peaceful in life. Choosing a spiritual way of life with or without religion will bring a holistic approach to life, which, in turn, brings love, compassion and happiness.

"I am deeply thankful for your time and the elaborate discussions on choices and balance. Do you want me to think about any new idea so that I can collect my thoughts and come and meet you next week?"

"Thank you for spending some time with me; next time when we meet, we may perhaps discuss 'Yoga and Meditation'. You may, therefore, reflect on this matter and when we meet we will find out what relevance it has in the present modern life. Good day."

CHAPTER 8

Yoga And Meditation

*Yoga teaches us to cure what need not be endured and
endure what cannot be cured.*

B.K.S. Iyengar

"Good morning. I am pleased to see you today. Last time I met you, you asked me to contemplate on 'yoga and meditation' before I come to meet you. I did contemplate. But you know I got into a serious muddle. I don't know which way I have to proceed. Could you please help me?" the young one asked when he met the old one.

"Good morning. I am very happy to see you today. I wonder what you mean by muddle."

"In popular view, everyone is talking about yoga and meditation as if it has come as a newfound panacea for every sickness and suffering. Every street corner there is some yoga school or other. It keeps on advertising extravagantly to attract people to come and learn yoga and meditation. Such schools charge extravagantly as well. It happens all over the world. One can find them in any city such as New York, Los Angeles, Washington, Tokyo, London, Mumbai, New Delhi, Chennai etc. and also in other big towns in the world. Thousands of books and articles are being written. Audio C.Ds and VVDs are being made available everywhere. Also, people talk about different kinds of yoga and meditative practices with different meanings. I do not know which one I should choose. I am sorry to say that I am in a confused state of mind. May I seek your help?"

"You are right. I must tell you first, the meaning of yoga and meditation. Yoga is a Sanskrit word now finds a place in the Oxford Dictionary.

The word yoga is derived from the Sanskrit root 'yuj', which means 'to unite, to join, to add'. Yoga is the union of the body, the mind, and the spirit.

Meditation means to focus with mindfulness of breathing to calm the mind.

> "The rhythm of the body, the melody of the mind, and the harmony of the soul create the symphony of life".
>
> **B.K.S. Iyengar**

Some say that yoga and meditation is now going to India, its place of birth in a big way. In its new avatar it has embraced many kinds of different schools of yoga and meditative practices of different parts of the world. Also, it is true to a large extent that there is now a great deal of awareness among people in the whole world. In any big department store or small store anywhere in the world one will find yoga mats which are now being sold as essential household items for families. But the fact remains that it is a way of life to learn to be in a relaxed manner, breathe in a natural way and stay harmoniously with the nature by uniting the body, the mind, and the spirit in asanas (postures) and breathing with mindfulness.

"This is what that confuses me. First, is there any simple way to understand and then practice yoga and meditation?

"You want everything in a quick-fix and ready to cook fashion. However, I will try to explain it as simple as possible. But it is purely left to you to catch up and practice in your own way. It is better to know the historical perspective of yoga and meditation. This will help the present generation to understand that this system is time tested by thousands of years and validated by the cotemporary science. The Vedas in India from time immemorial discussed yoga and meditation. Later, more than 5000 years ago, seers and rishis in India continued to practice in the Himalayan Mountains. A large or countless number of yogis is still continuing to practice in the Himalayas.

Through their numerous disciples, they carried their experiential practices from time to time to common people not only in India, but also in various countries such as Greece, Afghanistan, Middle East, Tibet,

Myanmar, Thailand, Cambodia, Laos, Sri Lanka, China, Korea, Vietnam, and Japan. Bodhi Dharma, a prince from Kancheepuram, in South India took it to China. It became 'ch'an' in China. When it went to Korea, it became 'san' and it became 'zen' in Japan. Shankara, Ramanuja, Rama Krishna Paramahamsa, Vivekananda, Aurobindo, Ramana Maharishi followed the practices in their pursuit of divine happiness.

Vivekananda, as early as 1893, went to U.S.A to attend the World Congress of Religions held in Chicago on September, 11, 1893. When he rose to address the audience in the conference and said "Sisters and brothers of America" in his opening remark, 7,000 people in the audience, immediately feeling the depth of his sincerity, rose to their feet and according to reports, "went into inexplicable rapture with standing ovation and clapping that lasted for more than three minutes."

He later went on lecturing on traditional yoga and meditation in different parts of USA and other Western countries. His lectures attracted the attention of millions of people all over the world. Later, Maharishi Mahesh Yogi, Swami Rama, Paramahamsa Yogananda, Swami Satchidananda and a host of other yogis carried the practices and promoted them in the Western world.

Similarly, monks from Japan, Tibet, Vietnam, and other countries and also scholars, educationists from various parts of the world kept on visiting western countries and spread the principles and practices of yoga and meditation in different forms through the various universities and ashrams besides lectures and seminars. In contemporary times, some of the most renowned monks and scholars like His Holiness Dalai Lama, Thich Nhat Hanh, Dr. D.T.Suzuki, Chogyam Tungpa and many others are continuing to spread the messages of yoga and meditation of different kind of their own faiths and beliefs for the whole world.

Today, yoga and meditation are practiced on a daily basis by millions of people in every country of the world. The number is increasing year by year as the awareness goes up day by day."

"The Vedas, Upanishads, Bhagavad Gita and the other scriptures discussed yoga and meditation in a very detailed manner. The Yoga Vasishtha, consisting of 32000 verses, is believed to have preceded the

Bhagavad Gita. While Jnana Yoga and Karma Yoga are highlighted in Yoga Vasishtha, Bhakti Yoga is included along with Jnana Yoga and Karma Yoga and detailed in Bhagavad Gita.

However, about 2000 years ago, Maharishi Patanjali codified in a poetic and classical way the practices of yoga in his Yoga Sutra. It is a masterpiece in Sanskrit. It contains 195 sutras (aphorisms). They are very concise and loaded with powerful insight in the form of sutras. All of them very briefly lay out the meaning and direction of yoga and meditation and the connection between the mind, the body and the spirit or soul."

"May I now request you to tell me about yoga and meditation in a simple way so that I can understand without any confusion in my mind?"

"To answer you and to start with, this is what Mariel Hemingway said about yoga and meditation:

"I wanted to share the experience of how yoga and meditation have transformed my life, how they have enabled me to observe who I am, first in my body, and then emotionally, and on to a kind of spiritual path."

Yoga and meditation are like two eyes. Only with the help of the two, one can reach the level of natural state of being. But in popular terms, yoga is generally understood as vigorous exercise or twisting or lifting or bending the limbs of the body or simply asanas (postures).Yoga nowadays has become synonymous with asanas. Asana is only one limb of yoga. Asana is looked at as a posture rather than its original meaning of "a state of being". One experiences and evokes many qualities and aspects from within. Sthiram (stability and firmness) Sukham (comfort and ease) Asanam (movement of limbs) is what Patanjali says in his Yoga Sutras.

Similarly, meditation is generally understood only as yogic practices intended for yogis or simply 'breathing exercises'. Truly, both are to be unified and practiced together.

Yogasanas—movements of the limbs of the body—yoga, should be unified with meditation—the regulated breathing—inhaling and exhaling diaphragmatically with the focus of the mind—meditation.

Fundamentally, body and mind should be focused together to breathe naturally and 'still' the mind from constant chattering. In the second sutra in Yoga Sutra, Patanjali says, 'yoga chitta vritthi nirodhah'. It means that the mind should be still to focus and sustain from distractions."

"Is that simple and easy? I repeatedly try. But every time I try, all kinds of thoughts cloud my mind and distract me from proceeding further. What shall I do to still the mind?" In what way will it help anyone in the present day of ever changing hectic way of life which throws up new kind of health problems on an increased level such as stress, strain, heart problems, memory loss, anxiety and depression?"

"You are right. It is said that 'the meditation is simple in concept, but difficult to master'. The mind constantly produces thoughts like waves in the ocean. The mind, in every fraction of a second, is made to jump from one thought to another like monkeys jumping from one branch to another in a tree. However if one learns the theory and practices it regularly with commitment and passion then it will become a habit which will train the mind and body to still the mind automatically. If one tries for a week or a month and leaves it thereafter, then nothing will happen. There are six cardinal points which are important to achieve best results.

understanding,
determination,
preparation,
practice,
regularity,
continuity.

"Whatever forms of meditation you practice, the most important point is to apply mindfulness continuously, and make a sustained effort. It is unrealistic to expect results from meditation within a short period of time. What is required is continuous sustained effort."

His Holiness Dalai Lama

To put it simply one should sit quietly in the open or in a room. The mind and the body should be kept in total relaxation. The place should be such that there should not be any distractions which will affect the quietness of the place and disturb the mind. Now, one should close the eyes and focus on a word or mantra, or a picture which is familiar to the mind by visualization. Slowly and gently inhaling and exhaling diaphragmatically should be undertaken with the focus and mindfulness of the breathing. If any thought comes in the way one should allow it to pass through the mind and resume back again inhaling and exhaling. No force should be exerted to change the thoughts.

Now, one can start counting the inhaling and exhaling. To start with one can inhale 2 counts then the exhaling should follow for 4 counts. Likewise the inhaling and exhaling can be increased from 3 to 6 and 4 to 8 respectively and so on.

The mind gets engaged with the focus on an object with inhaling and exhaling with mindfulness and with counts. When all these are done together at a time the mind slowly gets stilled and the state of being achieved.

In recent times, Dr. Herbert Benson M.D. Harvard Medical School with his associates made a lot of research on meditation to begin with Transcendental Meditation of Maharishi Mahesh Yogi and finally introduced in 1975 a simple mind-body approach to relieve stress.

He called it as 'The Relaxation Response' meditation which attracted the attention of millions in the world.

Now, it has become the most researched techniques of meditation. According to this technique one will have to simply focus on a word or a phrase or God as you breathe slowly and deeply. This will make one to feel quiet, calm, focused, and peaceful. This is a simple and effective kind of meditation. It takes a few minutes to learn and a few minutes more to practice. It is reported that this type of meditation is used in hundreds of stress reduction programmes throughout U.S.A. and other countries.

It is found out by research that 'The Relaxation Response' meditation generates neurological and psychological states of serenity and health.

This meditation practice is now being routinely recommended by doctors and health care professionals to treat patients suffering from heart conditions, chronic pain, high blood pressure, insomnia, and other physical pains.

Many medical Schools and other Schools adopted yoga and meditation in their curriculum. Cardiologists and other Doctors use yoga and meditation to help patients to get quick healing before and after surgery. Physiotherapists use yoga techniques in helping patients to get their body pains healed.

As late as in 2009, Andrew Newberg M.D, and Mark Robert Waldman in their path breaking book, 'How God Changes Your Brain' have explained how meditation and yoga changes the brain.

They made specific research on how gentle form of yoga and meditation will help people suffering from memory problems.

> "Meditation allows us to change our brains, bodies,
> and state of being".
>
> **Dr. Joe Dispenza**

"Thanks. However, I would like to know how mantra comes into the system of yoga and meditation and why?"

The universe, the body, other animate and inanimate things are energy in vibration. They are made up of atoms and molecules, which are essentially wave forms. Words and sounds are also energy in vibrations. As they are interconnected, words and sounds can influence body and mind. These are recent findings of various researches made in U.S.A and other Western countries.

Mantra is a Sanskrit word and it is power packed. It had been recorded and reported in many scriptures that the mantras are found to be effective in healing the human body physically and in healing the mind in stilling and quietening.

Dr. Masaru Emoto, author of the Book, "Messages in Water", explained that, "the language, the spoken word, has a vibration. Written words also have vibration. Anything in existence has a vibration. If I were to draw a circle, the vibration of a circle would be created . . . . . . .Also, he explains how sounds influence the water and since the human body is made up of 75 per cent water, sounds that influence water influence the body."

Mantras when used in yoga and meditation along with mild movements of limbs with slow and steady breathing will help to still the mind and lift the body to a higher level of wellbeing.

It is reported from the researches made recently that hormones and neurotransmitters in our body communicate with each other through distinctive vibrational sympathise.

Besides the physical nervous system, it is also reported that there are 72,000 naadis (channels of energy). When mantra is chanted, the vibrational energy gets distributed into the physical nervous system by naadis through major chakras such as 1. Sahasrara (crown chakra), 2 Ajna. (brow chakra), 3.Visuddha(throat chakra), 4. Anahata (heart chakra), 5. Manipura (solar plexus chakra), 6. Swasdhisthana (Sacral chakra), and 7. Muladhara(Root chakra), i.e. centres of energy in the spinal column.

"After listening to you I am now clear that I should start practicing yoga and meditation immediately. Please tell me now how an ordinary person like me can learn and practice yoga and meditation in a systematic manner to derive maximum benefits?"

"You seem to be in a hurry to commence yoga and meditation. To begin, one should ensure that the body and mind should be kept in a relaxed position. No force should be applied. No pain or tension should be felt. Then the preparation, in nutshell, may have to be undertaken:

1) Early morning hours and evening hours are ideal.
2) Empty stomach should be ensured.
3) Sit quietly in an undisturbed room or a place without any distractions.
4) Sit in a padmasana posture (cross-legged with the palms up resting comfortably on the laps).
5) Sit erect with the spine in straight line.

6) Close the eyes and try to still the mind without any thoughts.
7) Focus on the word 'OM' or an object such as sun, moon, or an image like Christ, Buddha, Mohammed, Ganesha or any other object with which one is familiar.
8) Inhale and exhale with mindfulness. (One may keep counting when inhaling and also when exhaling). To start with, if one inhales for 2 counts, one should exhale for 4 counts.
9) When thoughts try to distract your mind away from focus on the object, do not exert force, but allow the thoughts to flow and bring the mind back to the object again.
10) Continue the practice to begin with 5 minutes and slowly increase to 10 minutes or more.
11) Practice in the same place and also in the same time as far as possible.
12) When repeated again and again, one will experience a sense of full awareness of peace, joy, sensation, alertness and quietness.

I must say that initially one should find a guide or mentor or teacher to learn yoga and meditation and later on one can continue to practice on his own in his home. "

"Sorry to interrupt. Is it necessary to prepare oneself every time? People talk of different kinds of yoga and meditation practices. They also talk about Walking Meditation, Eating Meditation, Singing Meditation, Reading Meditation and many other kinds. It is also said that at any time one can, according to his convenience, practice yoga and meditation. This is where I totally get lost and also confused. Could you please get me out of this confusion?"

"Preparation is a must. Principles and regularity are to be observed. Both are important to achieve maximum benefits. There is no doubt that there are many kinds. As I said earlier, the traditional Yoga Meditation is the mother of all practices. Others are variants of the original in different forms.

What we are talking about here is the secular one, which need not be associated with any particular region, religion or sect.

To make it clear, I must say that different countries i.e. India, Tibet, China, Japan, Sri Lanka, Vietnam, Korea, Myanmar and other countries follow different methods and practices. Similarly, different religions—Hinduism, Jainism, Buddhism, Christianity, Zoroastrianism, Islam, Judaism and other religions follow different methods and practices. Even in the postures—asanas—different kinds are followed.

Similarly, in the breathing practices too, different methods are being followed. Whatever is the method or kind, the core point is focus and natural breathing. Therefore, one should select the practice that suits him or her well. In this, the teacher will play a vital role."

"What do you mean by natural breathing? Also, why do you keep saying that guide or mentor or teacher is necessary when books and VVDs are available?

"When the child is born, no one teaches the child how to breathe, but the child picks up breathing in the natural way. When the child breathes, its stomach rises. This is called natural breathing. When the same child grows, the life's challenges, stress, strain, ambition, anger, jealousy, sorrow, suffering, losses, excitement etc. alter the natural breathing into the shallow breathing. Repeated incidences of shallow breathing result in habit formation. It is said that habit never dies.

Once the habit is formed then it becomes automatically routine and normal whether one likes it or not. The habit once becomes normal then the humans ignore it. That is how the shallow breathing has come to stay with the many humans. Most of us fall into this shallow breathing day in, day out, knowingly or unknowingly resulting in sickness, pain, agony, suffering, dullness and unhappiness in life.

Books and VVDs may help. But there are certain subtleties in practicing yoga and meditation which can be explained physically by the teacher. Also one will tend to commit mistakes in practicing yoga and meditation after learning from reading books or seeing others doing in VVDs.

For example to learn breathing diaphragmatically needs one to see physically when the guide does it for the student. Again when breathing, one will tend to raise the shoulders unconsciously. This over time may result in shoulder pain. Similarly there are a number of aspects which may look simple but will have to be explained explicitly and also corrections will have to be made periodically by the teacher.

Further the books and VVDs show photographs and explain in general the practices for everyone. But in reality each one may have some kind of health problems such as vertigo, giddiness, back pain, shoulder pain, abdominal pain, hernia etc. or might have gone through minor or major surgeries besides the individual's age.

These factors will have to be considered before anyone starts practicing yoga and meditation.

If one approaches a teacher to learn yoga and meditation, he will structure the type of yoga and meditation practices to suit one's own requirements after taking into consideration of all these factors and monitor with corrections whenever required. This will yield long time benefit and help to heal pain and suffering.

You know, gym enthusiasts, initially in their energetic eagerness and competitive urge, buy out whatever gym's machines available in the soaring market and stuff all of them in their homes. They try out the exercises one by one on the machines with the help of the instructions book. After sometime, they notice new found pains in the joints, shoulders, hip, back, and knees etc. which they had not experienced earlier.

Suddenly they close down the home gym and start visiting gym's centers to continue with the help of the trainers of the gym. Gym exercises will help to build muscles. It will not help to get total relaxation, calmness and lightness of the body and the mind. After a few months, they feel bored, exhausted, and get into fatigue syndrome which drives them to quit. Having their initial eagerness and enthusiasm receded, they discard the exercises once and for all.

Sam was one who had suffered knee pain and back pain due to misguided gym practices. Arthur was another who indulged in self help heavy weight lifting practices resulting in hernia operation at the age forty five. Two very well known personalities of literary world have written about the problems of pain when they practiced gym exercises for a number of years. With proper trainer and guidance gym will help but caution is necessary to safeguard one's health.

If you take yoga and meditation, the people who take to it with mindfulness, continue to realize total relaxation, calmness, lightness, and flexibility of the body and the mind. It is beneficial not only to the body but also to the mind. They also notice relief from the pains in joints, back, and hip etc. if they had any of those earlier. Further, it is the convenient, affordable, without any side effects, and easy to continue at home after learning initially from the teacher without using any expensive machines and other devices. Some do both to get benefits from both the practices.

"Sorry to interrupt again. Why is natural breathing so important in a day-to-day life?"

"It is called 'prana', the vital force and life's energy. If prana is not there, the body becomes a corpse. Whether one likes it or not, one keeps breathing to be alive. But, when one breathes correctly, which is achievable by regular yoga and meditation, one gets energy, focus, memory, clarity, vitality, peace, calmness and good health.

A large number of medical scientific research studies made in the USA and other European countries recently proved conclusively that regular practices of yoga and meditation help to maintain the heartbeat and the pulse rate correctly even in extreme conditions.

A Lama, when put into full body scan with different extreme conditions with his yoga and meditation, validated the findings in a laboratory in the USA as per the initiative taken by His Highness Dalai Lama.

"May I know now some simple methods of yoga and meditation?"

"One can easily practice Padmasana, Makarasana and Shavasana."

Padmasana—lotus posture—is the mother of all postures. Sit upright on the side bones, spine straight, legs intertwined, fingers interlaced, hands palms up, resting comfortably on the lap and eyes closed Now, breathe diaphragmatically i.e. inhaling and exhaling with the focus of the mind on the chosen object with mindfulness. To start with uniform breathing with equal length of inhaling and exhaling may be attempted. When the practice is stabilized, one can increase the length of inhaling 2, 3 and 4 or more counts and exhaling 4, 6 and 8 counts.

"Makarasana—Crocodile Posture—Lie down face prone on the floor. Keep your crossed folded hands below the head, palms resting on the shoulders. Stretch the legs as far as possible, toes pointing outwards. Relax in this posture for two to three minutes, with normal breathing.

It should flow like a smooth stream. Observe the gentle flow along with the rise and fall of the stomach and the naval area. Constantly take note of the breathing process. To start with, do the practice for 5 minutes, which may be increased to 10 to 15 minutes or more.

"Shavasana—Corpse Posture—lie on the back stretching the legs apart, facing the ceiling or sky. The hands should be kept and stretched by the side of the body with the palms up.

Now breathe with regular inhaling and exhaling closing the eyes. Relax completely without any strain or pain. Relax for 1 minute or more."

"I am deeply indebted for your discourse. Can I straight away start the practice?"

"No. What we discussed is only the theory. For practice, as I said earlier, one should find a guide or a mentor or a teacher. From elementary school onwards up to PhD or even later in life, one always finds a guide or a mentor or a teacher to learn. Similarly, yoga and meditation should also be learnt through a guide or a mentor or a teacher. In the system of yoga and meditation, there is no distant learning.

"Let me now tell you about Pranayama. Prana means the life force and vital energy. Ayama means to regulate or to control or to retain.

Pranayama

   (a) Close the right nostril with the right thumb and inhale through the left nostril. Do this for 4 counts.
   (b) Immediately close the left nostril with your right hand middle finger and at the same time remove your right thumb from your right nostril and exhale through the right nostril. Do this for 8 counts. This completes a half round.

107

(c) Inhale through the right nostril after closing the left nostril for 4 counts. Immediately close the right nostril and exhale through the left nostril for 8 counts. This completes one full round. Start with 3 to 4 rounds and gradually increase the rounds.

One can do these practices twice a day. If not, at least once a day regularly. I tried to avoid all Sanskrit words and different kinds and methods of yoga and meditation practices to make this dialogue as simple as possible. Whatever be the kind and method of yoga and meditation one chooses to follow the fact remains that yoga and meditation is the best healthy way of living one can have in one's life.

> "The gift of learning to meditate is the greatest gift you can give yourself in this lifetime."
>
> **Sogyal Rinpoche**

"I must thank you for your elaborate exposition with a lot of patience with me. May I request you to tell me at least the names of those different kinds and methods?"

"There are many, such as Transcendental Meditation, Vipasana Meditation, Tao Meditation, Zen Meditation, Classical Vedantic Meditation, Tantra Meditation, and Mindfulness Meditation and so on. In this context, I would like to tell you a Zen story.

Once a student, after learning the basics of yoga and meditation, asked his Zen master how he has achieved such an elevated position in yoga and meditation. The Zen master replied:

> "while I work, I work mindfully,
> while I eat, I eat mindfully,
> and while I sleep, I sleep mindfully".

This explains all your doubts. Thanks for your patient hearing. Next time when you meet me, please come after meditating on 'Purpose and Meaning of Life.' Good day.

CHAPTER 9

The Purpose And Meaning Of Life

"As far as we can discern, the sole purpose of human existence is to kindle a light of meaning in the darkness of mere being."

Carl Jung

"*Good morning. I am very happy to meet you today. First, I thank you for giving me time to continue our dialogue. Last time I met you, you asked me to meditate on 'what is the purpose and meaning of life.' and meet you with my findings. I have come with my empty mind. To me, it appears that there is neither a purpose nor meaning of life. Each one leads a life as it comes and goes when it ends,*" the young one told the old one.

"You put it in a very simplistic way. Do you really feel so?"

"*Yes. I applied my mind and closely watched the way people live their lives and come to this conclusion. If you ask any ordinary person, he will say that the life itself is a struggle and where is the time to think of the purpose and meaning of life.*"

"On the superficial way you look at the life when it unfolds itself, you may tend to think on those lines. But if you try to understand that besides the physical self, there is something inside everyone that makes one feel, emote, understand, realize, think, remember and recall the events; then perhaps one may realize that there are two sides for everyone.

The one is physical self and the other is inner self. The physical self is visible. The inner self is invisible. You may even say that the inner self is the operating system that operates the physical self.

Generally, humans try to do thousand and one things either for mere survival or for success in life without having any purpose and meaning. In such a situation, one chooses to lead a life as it comes in whatever place one is landed in life either by circumstances or unexpected incidents. In these circumstances every one tends to become bitter and unhappy. In the words of Parkhurst Charles H, "Purpose is what gives life a meaning." The only way to find the purpose and meaning of life is to understand the self-awareness.

Professor V.S. Ramachandran in his path breaking book, 'The Tell—Tale Brain', says, that " . . . the self is aware of itself; it can contemplate its own existence and alas its mortality. He goes on to say that "Self-awareness is a trait that not only makes us human but also paradoxically makes us want to be more than merely human." The inner self always try to look for higher or elevated aspirations beyond the mundane and survival instincts of humans. Unless ignored or suppressed by the pressure and strains of day to day life, it tries to lift the spirit of every human irrespective of the place or occupation in which one is placed in life to higher levels of living one's life.

> "No man or woman is an island. To exist just for yourself is meaningless. You can achieve the most satisfaction when you feel related to some greater purpose in life something greater than yourself".
>
> **Denis Waitley**

"Sorry. I am getting more confused. If you say physical self, I can understand that you mean the body. But when you say inner self, I will not be able to understand. Why should I worry about something that is not visible? When everyone has enormous problems to face in everyday life, where is the need to understand something that is not visible to anyone?"

"There are many invisible matters, such as the spirit, God, human feelings, thoughts and emotions. One cannot say that they are not important because they are not visible. This is the mystery of creation. Duality in everything is part of existence. If you take nature, hot and cold, day and night, sun and moon, water and fire are duality in visible terms.

If you take humans, happiness and sorrow, love and hate, belief and non-belief are duality in invisible terms. Similarly, visible and invisible, form and no form are duality in nature. Therefore, it is necessary that one should understand that there is a physical self and an inner self in everyone. The inner self although invisible, plays a vital role in everyday life. In this context I remember what Antoine de Saint Exupery once wrote, "It is only with the heart one can see rightly; what is essential is invisible to the eye." You also said about problems. Even the problems are understood not by the body, but by the mind and the self."

"If self is important, why people do not give importance to it?"

"Like body, the self exists within the body itself. Whether one gives importance or not, it functions, without one's recognition or awareness. Richard Bach wrote that, "Your obligation in any life time is to discover the self." It is important only to humans to understand the self, its nature and to keep the awareness intact to hear its voice and take its guidance to live a life with a purpose and meaning. In this context it is important to know what J. Krishnamurti said once. He said that, "I must become aware of the total field of my own self which is the consciousness of the individual and of the society. It is only then, when the mind goes beyond the individual and social consciousness, that I can become a light to myself that never goes out."

"How can one first determine the purpose and thereafter the meaning of life so that one can understand the role of the self?"

"Awareness is important. Self-awareness leads to understand the inner meaning of every action. When one is aware that the self makes one feel, emote, realize, store in memory, recall the memories and react to those memories, one can realize how one's life is scripted and unfolded by the self. Immanuel Kant said that "The greatest human quest is to know what one must do in order to become a human being."

"You mean to say that one can shape the purpose and the meaning of life by taking control of the self?"

"It is not control. It is the awareness and understanding. In the words of Ouspensky, "To remember oneself means the same thing as to be aware of oneself—I am. It is not a function, not thinking, not feeling; it is a different state of consciousness."

It will help to lay a path. To put it differently, I would say that to lay a path of purpose and meaning of life, one need to take care of . . .

> Self-awareness,
> feelings,
> emotions,
> realization,
> intentionality,
> memories,
> values,
> what to achieve,
> where to go,
> ultimate goal

"May I now request you to explain one by one for my understanding?"

"Yes, I will do".

SELF-AWARENESS

"Self plays a vital role. If one understands the authentic self, one can slowly nurture and sustain the self that, in turn, will become the guide for one's life. For example, everyone tends to think that the purpose of life is to make money, wealth, acquire as much as material possessions, power, fame and relationships, which ultimately lead to happiness. In reality, it is not true; these are only the means and not the end. When one gets confused with the means as the end, then, as you said earlier, the problems and conflicts arise. These are the means of purpose and the end is the meaning of life.

When one recognizes the power of the self, the self will analyze and guide to reach the correct destination, i.e. meaning of life.

FEELINGS

"In everyday life, one is impacted by many kinds of feelings. These feelings arise in one's interactions with oneself, family members, friends, relatives, office workers and society at large. Negative feelings always sap the energy. They create negative vibrations all over, which in turn, returns to the same person and impacts in a vicious circle. Negative feelings, such as failure syndrome, low esteem, lack of self-confidence, laziness, low level of energy and self-defeating attitudes will make the self-suffer. This suffering, in turn, manifests in the form of sickness, failures, withdrawal syndrome and unhappiness.

On the other hand, if one cultivates positive feelings and directs the self to respond, the self will make one achieve whatever purpose for which one exists. The positive feelings, such as high esteem, intention to achieve, high confidence level and high level of energy, appreciation, enthusiasm, love and commitment will make the self to achieve whatever one intends to achieve.

"May I interrupt? Does it mean that the self by itself will not help humans?"

"As I told earlier, there should be awareness of the self. The self by itself is invisible and feeble. It requires awareness to identify, cultivate and listen. It will certainly be showing signs and sounding alarms at times. But it is always up to the humans to pick up the self's voices and also make them louder so that one will not miss out.

"Thanks; you may please proceed."

EMOTIONS

"Emotions like anger, jealousy, fear, envy, and hatred are self-destructive. On the other hand, love, compassion, loving kindness, acceptance, expressive appreciation and willingness to share will energize the self and help to achieve the purpose of life.

REALIZATIONS

Like awareness, the realization of the existential potentialities and the infinite opportunities provided by nature should be again and again reinforced in the self. Also, realization of one's own strengths and weaknesses along with the lessons of life's experiences will add to the strength to proceed on a successful journey of life with purpose and meaning.

INTENTIONALITY

The intention to achieve the purpose and the meaning of life will have to be regained every day. The power of intention will be realized only when the results are achieved. The self will help when the intention is intensified to achieve the result.

MEMORIES

The memories of the past will follow like the shadows. Although old memories could not be avoided, one should always cultivate to remember the pleasant and the glorious incidents of the past that will induce the self to achieve pleasant purposes in life. Bad memories should be dealt with like diseases and the self will have to be protected from the evil effects of the bad incidents of the past.

THE VALUES

The values in human life will have to be reinforced time and again so that one should not slip away from them at any point of time. The self will always intend to protect the identified values by humans. The values like happiness, peace, joy, celebrations, work, creating, sustaining, protecting, togetherness, live and let live, co-operation, co-existence, universal love and compassion will have to be identified, nurtured and sustained to achieve the purpose and meaning of life.

WHAT TO ACHIEVE, WHERE TO GO

What to achieve in life may differ from person to person; also the nature, the capability, the environment in which one lives, the systems of education, governance, health and society will play important roles. But, in general terms, the achievements alone cannot be considered as the purpose and meaning of life. They will depend on fulfillment, joy, peace and enduring happiness. One may be a carpenter, farmer, industrial worker, poet, philosopher, leader, priest, chairman of companies, executive and so on. If one aims at performing at one's highest level, it will give fulfillment in life. Similarly, the same path where one gets fulfillment will lead the self to the destination—the end, i.e. the meaning of life. In nobler and laudable terms Joseph Campbell said that, "The goal of life is to make your heart beat match the beat of the universe, to match your nature with Nature".

ULTIMATE GOAL

One should have the ultimate goal in life so that one can use all the means at one's command to meet the purpose and the meaning of life. The means in addition to what we have discussed so far are . . ."

CO-CREATION

Humans are co-creators with nature's creative intelligence-God. In the Law Of Nature co-creating, multiplying, sustaining, growing, withering, dissolving, and re-creating and continuing the process of life are the essential functions of its core aspect. Humans play a vital role as a predominant functionary not only in co-creating but also in the process of evolution in providing and safe guarding ecology for the existence of life system in our lonely planet. However humans sometimes take extreme actions in safe guarding their own self-interests using their extraordinary power of intelligence in the development of science and technology. To meet the growing demands of their own tribes they manipulate the creative nature of animals, birds, food grains, and vegetables, fruits and so on in their size, quality, and also multiply their growth in most unnatural ways and means.

But when it comes to their own existence they not only limit their co-creation but also try to reach zero point of population growth. These approaches and practices create imbalances and conflicts in the humans' lives such as social, environmental, and even health problems. In most countries children are treated as the properties of parents. In some advanced countries they are treated as the properties of the state. But the truth is:

"Your children are not your children
they are the sons and daughters
of life's longing for itself";

Kahlil Gibran

CONTRIBUTION

Humans also contribute along with the nature to create assets, wealth and other material objects and also contribute to others and their lives. Every one intentionally and sometimes unintentionally contributes to others for their welfare, development, progress, and to lead a life of comfort and satisfaction. Such deeds make one stands out in the crowd.

RECEIVING

Humans receive enormous benefits from the nature and also from others including other humans to live their lives.

"A hundred times every day I remind myself that my inner
and outer life depend on labors of other men living and
dead, and that I must exert myself in order to give in the
same measure as I have received and am still receiving."

Albert Einstein

GIVING

Humans in normal existence give and exchange whatever they produce for the sustenance and the multiplication of the natural products and services. But this is nothing but arising out of survival instinct of the individual and also of other humans. But they also provide help physically, mentally, financially and spiritually to others who are in need of such help which is of high order of existence. Giving always remains the core aspect of human existence in its noble form. In giving lies the joy of living. The 'joy of giving' movement is slowly gaining ground. Service to others is the supportiveness of living.

The rich people slowly realize that they are not only the sole owners of their wealth but also the trustees of such wealth on behalf of others who contribute directly or indirectly to create their wealth. This lofty idea helps them to give and share their wealth with others who are in need of such giving and sharing. Lao Tzu says in the book, 'Hua Hu Ching' that "Supportiveness manifests as service to others without expectation of reward or even a thank you—it is the quintessential component of feeling that life has a purpose

RESPONSIBILITY

Humans have a responsibility to save, sustain and protect the planet on which they are temporary residents.

When all these means are carefully and purposefully used by humans, as individuals, families, communities, societies and nations, the realization of the individual's ends will become easier to achieve.

SPIRITUAL AWAKENING

Finally, spiritual awakening will help one to find the meaning in one's life. In the words of D.T.Suzuki, "Awakening is no other than consciousness becoming acquainted with itself. "

> "The one possible way of giving meaning to (man's) existence is that of raising his natural relation to the world to a spiritual one."
>
> **Albert Schweitzer**

To sum up I would like to quote finally what Swami Vivekananda said: "Get up, and set your shoulder to the wheel—How long is this life for? As you have come into this world, leave some mark behind. Otherwise, where is the difference between you and the trees and stones? They too come into existence, decay and die."

"Thanks; your discussion was enlightening. I am deeply indebted to you. I now feel I am on the correct path, which will take me safely to my destination in life."

"Thanks for your patient hearing. Perhaps, when we meet tomorrow, we may ponder over on 'Magical Pathways'. You may, therefore, reflect on the valuable Magical Pathways which are laid out in front of us and let us put our minds together and understand what they are and how they work for uplifting the humans, when we meet tomorrow. Good day."

CHAPTER 10

Magical Pathways

"There's something magical about putting yourself into life.
You have got to stand up and take responsibility for your
own life and you cannot abandon that."

Bill Kurtis

"*Good morning. May I request you to take me on your path straightaway as I am going to observe silence and listen to you without interfering in your discourse today?*"

"I will do, but at least keep your ears open; the old one replied to the young one, and then he commenced his discourse. There are some extraordinary pathways which we call as magical pathways available for every human to take and proceed to find magical results on the way of life's journey and reach magical life at the destination. These magical pathways are valuable for shaping one's life and make it magical. These are evolved over a period of long time of human existence and time tested. However in present times, many humans tend to ignore them and find comforts in easy and rapidly changing fast life which leaves no time for them even to reflect on their own life and make shifts to healthy, happy, and purposeful way of life with meaning.

Instead of making the body and the mind work in harmony to take the magical pathways, every human is trying to search outside to make life magical. Why these magical pathways are ignored and not taken for life's journey and why many humans lead their lives with sickness, suffering, pain, misery, and unhappiness are the questions to which every generation is trying to find answers.

First one should understand the nature of the magical pathways before one takes the first step. Then one should continue the journey with mindfulness. Continuing with regularity and commitment will alone lead to the desired destination of magical life. "Knowing is not enough; we must apply. Willingness is not enough; we must do." This is what Johann Wolfgang von Goethe has said.

Each pathway is not magical by itself. But all the pathways lead to one destination which is magical. The magical results are health, peace, happiness, and wealth of leading a life of fulfillment all of which ultimately make one's life magical.

Perhaps the evolution of the mind and the realization of consciousness slowly help humans to understand the values of these magical pathways and make shifts to continue their life's journey on these magical pathways for life's fulfillment.

PATHWAY OF IMAGINATION

Imagination is one of the magical pathways. According to Ralph Waldo Emerson, "Imagination is a very high sort of seeing."

The positive, productive and creative imaginations will keep the mind fully occupied consciously and unconsciously. This will protect the mind from the unwanted and the undesired chattering. The right kind of imaginations will always help one to bring the goal in life from the invisible status to the reality status. If one locates and proceeds on this pathway, one can convert the imagination into reality. In his own enigmatic way George Bernard Shaw said that, "Imagination is the beginning of creation. You imagine what you wish for and you wish for what you imagine and finally end up creating what you wish for. Norman Vincent Peale said that "Imagination is the true magic carpet."

The poets, the writers and the achievers in sports, arts, professions and in various other human activities internalize their imaginations and bring out the best in their lives. William Blake wrote that, "What is now proved was once only imagined." This is the fundamental truth of imagination. In this context, what Albert Einstein said was far more relevant forever. He said that, "Imagination is more important than knowledge. For knowledge is limited to all we know now and understand, while imagination embraces the entire world, and all there ever will be to know and understand."

"To know is nothing at all; to imagine is everything."
Anatole France

PATHWAY OF DREAMS

Dreams of future are the milestones on the life's journey which lead one to the desired destination. Henry David Thoreau wrote that, "I learned at least this by my experiments. That if anyone advances confidently in the direction of his dreams and endeavors to live the life which he has imagined, he will meet with a success unexpected in common hours."

When dreams are internalized and focused with pure intentionality then they will become realities in one's life. Dreamers have become achievers in human history. George Bernard Shaw said that "You see things and you say 'why?'. But I dream things that never were; and I say 'why not?" Empty dreams are as useless as empty promises. Dreams of highest level of achievements and realizing lofty ideas in whatever place one has found himself in life will always materialize in reality if one pursues them with sincerity of purpose. Mahatma Gandhi's and Martin Luther King's dreams were of very high order and looked impractical to achieve in those difficult times of their lives. But they were achieved as they dreamed. If such extraordinary dreams were achieved by such simple and ordinary leaders, why ordinary dreams of ordinary humans could not be achieved?

This magical pathway appears naturally to every human. If one takes it and continues to walk through it with mindfulness, the magical results will happen not only on its sideways but also at the destination.

"A dream is your creative vision for your life in the future.
You must break out of your current comfort zone and
become comfortable with the unfamiliar and the unknown."
Denis Waitley

PATHWAY OF INTENTION

The pure intention inside and its vibration outside will impact the universe to conspire to result in achievement. Deepak Chopra wrote that "Intentions compressed into words unfold magical power." When the imaginations and the dreams are internalized in the form of pure intentions, the achievement becomes easier. The intention has its own power to energize the body and the mind to materialize it. Daniel G. Amen M.D. author of 'Change your Brain, Change your Life', says that "When our behaviors match our intentions, when our actions are equal to our thoughts, when our minds and our bodies are working together, when our words and deeds are aligned . . . there is immense power behind any individual." Every human experiences this power in his everyday life. The Zen teachings emphasize more on intention than action. Mahatma Gandhi said that, "Every moment of your life is infinitely creative and the universe is endlessly bountiful. Just put forth a clear enough request and everything your heart desires must come to you". This is the way the Law of Intentionality operates. This magical pathway may look as hidden. But when identified and taken it will easily lead to the destination of magical life.

> "Intentional living means
> what you do is one with what you are.
> Clarity of purpose, an open heart, and a lively mind
> gives us the power to direct our destinies.
> To live by choice and chance,
> this is what it is to live an intentional life."
> **Stuart Avery Gold**

PATHWAY OF ATTRACTION

"Like attracts like"; This Law of Attraction is more powerful. This law has to be recognized. Many may ignore it. When the signals of attraction are sent out subtly by humans, they, like magnets, attract similar persons, matters, energies, functions and results. The positive vibrations attract positive connections and results. The negative vibrations will attract negative connections and results. One should realize this aspect and accordingly one should proceed on this magical path for one's benefit.

> "The law of attraction, 'like attracts like'...
> No one lives beyond this law because
> it is the law of universe."
>
> **Lynn Grabhorn**

PATHWAY OF PRESENT

This magical pathway although appears to be obvious, is ignored in such a way that everyone always lives in the past and fears the future. The result is that many do not live in the present. When one is fully engaged in the past and the future, the present slips away quietly, leaving the burden of the past and fear of the future stuffed into the minds of humans. In Charles Dickens's words, "Reflect upon your present blessings, of which every man has plenty; not on your past misfortunes, of which all men have some." This path is the only path which will take one to the future and leaves the present behind and throws it into the past.

Alan Watts said that, "Memories of the past and anticipation of the future exist only now, and thus to try to live completely in the present is to strive for what already is the case." Whatever one does in the present is only important in one's life. This path which is called the present will have to be recognized and taken consciously to reach one's own fulfillment of the desired destination. In the words of Father Kallistos Ware "The present is the point where time touches eternity."

> "Yesterday is history. Tomorrow is a mystery.
> Today is a gift. That is why it is called
> 'the present'. Cherish it."
>
> **Spencer Johnson**

PATHWAY OF BELIEFS

This magical path is a hidden pathway. This is hidden in the hearts of humans from the very beginning. The beliefs are the cornerstones of every religion.

The beliefs have helped humans to achieve and heal themselves. Perhaps the fear of unknown must have played a vital role in the belief system of humans in the beginning of human life on our planet. But this hidden path, even in the 21st century, is being considered valuable. The scientific research study made on knee replacement both real and fake proved the effect on the healing by Dr. Bruce Moseley.

This kind of belief is known as placebo effect on medical treatment is slowly recognized by medical community all over the world.

> "Some people get better when they believe
> (falsely) they are getting medicine.
> When patients get better by ingesting a sugar pill,
> medicine defines it as the 'placebo effect'
> **Bruce H. Lipton, PH.D**

Dr. Eben Alexander, M.D. an academic neurosurgeon for the last 25 years, including 15 years at the Brigham & Women's and Children's Hospitals and Harvard Medical School in Boston, in his book, 'Proof of Heaven' published in 2012, in the course of detailing his near death experiences (NDEs), explains about the 'crucial power of belief in facilitating 'mind-over-matter'.

Slowly the medical profession has come to terms with the placebo effect and now it is well established that the ancient belief system plays a vital role in medical treatment as well as in other aspects of human life.

> "Seeing is not believing. Believing is seeing.
> You see things not as they are but as you are."
> **Erick Butterworth**

PATHWAY OF FAITH

This magical pathway is as old as humans. But, due to modern advancement in science and technology, one tends to ignore it. But human history reveals how the faith system like the belief system helped humans to achieve and heal not once, but in many times in one's life. Dr. Martin Luther King Jr. is assertive when he said that "Take the first step in faith. You do not have to see the whole staircase, just take the first step."

It is also true that faith has evolved itself into such a powerful tool in the hands of humans to realize what one wants to achieve in one's life time. Faith creates a sense of hope; hope in turn provides fodder for effort; effort finally results in achievement. In addition faith lifts everyone to a higher level of consciousness. It was Napoleon Hill in his book 'Outwitting the Devil' wrote that, "The state of mind known as faith apparently opens to one, the medium of a sixth sense through which one may communicate with sources of power and information far surpassing any available through the five physical senses."

Today, the modern scientists by the various researches made by them are slowly finding the effectiveness of faith in the life of humans. Faith, according to Andrew Newberg and Mark Robert Waldman as per their recent research findings say that, "Faith is essential for maintaining a healthy brain." Therefore one can say that the sincere and pure faith will always help humans to achieve and heal themselves in their life.

"What is faith? It is a state of mind wherein one recognizes and uses the power of positive thought as a medium by which one contacts and draws upon the universal store of Infinite Intelligence at will"

Napoleon Hill

PATHWAY OF PRAYER

Prayer is not a ritual. On the other hand, prayer, when it is done as a duty every day, will have a wonderful effect on the mind and spirit. This is, therefore, one of the ancient magical pathways that every religion has discovered and promoted for the well-being of humanity.

In prayer, one will always focus one's mind and slowly develop the skill to still the mind. In sincere and pure prayers one can experience the sensations or tingling in the body. When this concentration is achieved, the wishes in the forms of prayers are sent out loudly to the universe. The universe picks up the vibrations and help to ensure that they are materialized. This is what happens when people say that their prayers are answered.

People, therefore, develop self-confidence and their level of understanding and achievements improve. Prayers also open up the spiritual energy and reinforce the faiths and beliefs of the people to achieve their goals in life, whether it relates to health, wealth or happiness. Sometimes prayers by their power of focus and concentration create synchronicity, thereby seeing a situation one wants to see, meeting a person one dreams to see, encountering extraordinary opportunities all of a sudden, and experiencing success suddenly. When the Law of Synchronicity merges with the Law of Prayer, then magical occurrences will not become uncommon. This magical pathway is therefore magical in itself.

Napoleon Hill wrote that, "The person who goes to prayer with definiteness of purpose and faith in the attainment of that purpose puts into motion the laws of nature which transmute one's dominating desires into the physical equivalent. That is all there is to prayer."

"Visualize, prayerise and actualise."

Vincent Peale

PATHWAY OF YOGA AND MEDITATION

This is again an old magical pathway which has been hidden in the woods of humans' life's journey. This is truly a magical pathway which will have to be identified first and learnt properly from a teacher how to proceed on its path. In modern times, humans find more time to spend on many unproductive and unhealthy activities rather than a few minutes say 20 to 30 minutes every day on yoga and meditation. Yoga and meditation are somehow slowly regaining importance. The gains are proved scientifically now. Scientists, neurologists and cardiologists, by their research, say that yoga and meditation improves one's heart rate and help to reduce blood sugar, cholesterol and stress levels. The gains are many, such as clarity of mind, healthy perception of life and healthy heart and mind.

"The evidences of research made in universities
and medical institutions demonstrate that most
forms of contemplative meditation and yoga
will exercise your brain in ways that maintain
and promote cognitive health and vitality."

Andrew Newberg
Mark Robert Waldman

PATHWAY OF HUMILITY

Humility is the virtue that makes humans totally spiritual. Whenever the false self takes over the mind, humans become simply the mechanical body without a heart, soul and spirit. Such humans will not respect any other fellow traveler's feelings, emotions and knowledge. The ego centered mind makes one feel that he or she alone is great and the whole world should listen to him or her. Ultimately, the mind without humility leads one to loneliness, emptiness and self—destruction. Humility, therefore, will have to be cultivated and practiced without the feeling of self-pride and arrogance. When the scientist Einstein met the poet Rabindranath Tagore at his door step of his house in Germany and shook hands, he told his guest to his amazement that "I memorized a line of yours. ie. 'We come nearest to greatness when we are great in humility.' I believe it." Such is the power of humility which had united diametrically opposite two great minds of humanity.

The magical pathway of humility if one takes on his life's journey not only will help to experience magical results on the way but also lead to magical life as one's destination.

"Humility does not mean thinking less of yourself,
than of other people, nor does it mean having a
low opinion of your own gifts. It means freedom
from thinking about yourself at all."

William Temple

PATHWAY OF GRATITUDE

Gratitude is inner self's silent expression of feeling of thanksgiving. This magical pathway provides strengths and adds values on its path of humans' journey of life. It has got to be recognized as a virtue and consciously practiced in day-to-day way of life. If one says 'thanks' for every simple help one receives from others genuinely, the vibration of the feeling of good and happiness carries a wider vibration and will impact the other humans and the whole universe. These feelings of gratitude and the words arising out of such feelings and the deeds arising out of such words are the corner stones of happiness of human existence. Johannes A.Gaertner wrote that, "To speak gratitude is courteous and pleasant, to enact gratitude is generous and noble, but to live gratitude is to touch Heaven."

To help others at times of need and provide charity and service are meaningful expression of gratitude in one's pathway of life. It is mostly impossible to show gratitude to the same human who has provided help or support in any form in the same measure or in the same life time. One should therefore start from showing gratitude to the creative intelligence-God, parents, relatives, friends or whomsoever who are in need of any kind of service. This is a valuable treasure one should keep spending and by doing so one can realize that his vault containing this treasure will always be full to help to achieve more and more of one's dreams resulting in magical life.

> "I would maintain thanks are the highest form of thought;
> and that gratitude is happiness doubled by wonder."
> **G.K. Chesterton**

PATHWAY OF COMPASSION

Compassion is a noble way of living and a magical pathway which leads to a spiritual level of happiness. Unless one understands, feels, and practices by one's own reflection on life, it will be difficult for anyone to exercise it in day today life. Once it is realized that each one is not an island by one self and everyone is dependent on every other human and every other thing in the world in one way or other, even for mere existence, then one will develop the feeling of compassion towards others.

To be independent is one thing and understanding the interconnection with other human and every other thing in the world by the vibrations of feelings and emotions is another thing.

When one feels the pains and sufferings of others as one's own, then this kind of feeling evokes the loving kindness which one can call as compassion.

According to H. Jackson Brown Jr, "Compassion is the desire that moves the individual self to widen the scope of its self-concern to embrace the whole of the universal self."

Every day and every incident evokes some feeling or other in every human. If it happens to evoke a feeling of compassion, then the human being can be said to evolve herself into a real human with humane instinct in life.

"One of the basic points is kindness. With kindness, with love and compassion, with this feeling that is the essence of brotherhood, sisterhood, one will have inner peace. This compassionate feeling is the basis for inner peace."

His Holiness Dalai Lama

PATHWAY OF LOVE

Love is the spring of life. Love has the magnetic power of attraction. Love has the extraordinary creative power of life. Love can provide meaning and dignity of life to others. Love is the fountain of sacrifice. Love has no meaning for entitlement. Love is blind. Yes; it is blind to others' appearance, look, behavior, race, color, education, qualification, status, nationality, and gender. Love has no boundaries. Love embraces all as they are and enrich the life of others. Imposing one's will and authority have no meaning in love.

It was Rumi who said "Come out of the circle of time, and into the circle of love." Love is not to be identified or imposed but it is instantaneous not only in its nature but also in its approach. Prentice Mulford said that, "Love is an element which though physically unseen is as real as air or water ... It is acting, living, moving force .... it moves in waves and currents like those of the ocean."

Mother Teresa's life and work for humanity depended wholly on her love for destitute, dying, old, neglected humans, sick, and humans without any support from humanity just for day to day existence on account of their total incapacitation. She was an incarnation of love and compassion lived only to provide selfless service for the neglected and uncared humans by other humans. Once she said, "There is more hunger for love and appreciation in this world than for bread." This extraordinary magical pathway is heavenly in its nature and lifts the ordinary humans to the level of godliness in life.

"Through love all that is bitter will be sweet.
Through love all that is copper will be gold.
Through love all dregs will turn into the purest wine.
Through love all pain will turn into medicine."

RUMI

PATHWAY OF SERVICE

Service to individual, family, community, society, country, humanity, and ultimately the world is what every other human can provide in whatever place one is placed in life. But service is dependent only on selflessness. Many humans therefore stop with individual and family. Some may extend to community and society. Only extraordinary humans think of country, humanity and the world. Why this happens? The only reason one can think of is selfishness. Whosoever frees oneself from this bondage to a certain extent will be able to provide service to others. Albert Schweitzer wrote that, "There is no higher religion than human service. To work for the common good is the greatest creed."

The services to others may be of physical, financial, emotional, and spiritual. Sharing of happiness and sorrow is the essence of emotional service to others. There are other occupational, professional, and vocational services of enduring values which can be of great service to individual, community and society. Mahatma Gandhi said that, "Consciously or unconsciously, every one of us does render some service or other. If we cultivate the habit of doing this service deliberately, our desire for service will steadily grow stronger, and will make, not only our own happiness, but that of the world at large"

Knowing the exemplary lives of great and valiant savants of humanity will provide anyone the required urge and passion for service. Albert Einstein said that, "Only a life lived in service to others is worth living." This magical pathway will provide enduring happiness and everlasting fulfillment in life.

> "I slept and dreamt that life was joy.
> I woke and saw that life was service.
> I acted and behold, service was joy."
> **Rabindranath Tagore**

PATHWAY OF SIMPLICITY

Simplicity is not the opposite of extravagance only. It covers the entire spectrum of human activities. Starting from thoughts, words, and deeds it embraces every aspects of human life. One may think that it is easy for poor to be simple. Also for poor there will be no other option but to be simple. But it is not so. Poor or rich it makes no difference. One will have to consciously make efforts and formulate them as habits to be simple. Simplicity is the essence of effectiveness. When we say effectiveness, planning and time management etc. will not be substitutes for simplicity. On the other hand, simplicity will make effectiveness, planning and time management etc. easy and less stressful.

If one is simple in thoughts then the expression of thoughts will be easy not only for oneself but also for the other to understand and act. Similarly, if one makes his words simple both in conversation or in writing, then one can easily convey his thoughts or ideas and make them easily understandable by others. In the same way, if one makes his actions in simple way, then one will not make himself stressed out or give stress to others. Henry David Thoreau said that, "Our life is frittered away by detail. Simplify, simplify, simplify! I say, let your affairs be as two or three, and not a hundred or a thousand; instead of a million count half a dozen, and keep your accounts on your thumb-nail."

Mentally, physically, and materially also one will have to be simple in life. In the words of Leonardo da Vince, "Simplicity is the ultimate sophistication." If unwanted and undesired thoughts are not loaded in the mind, the mind will become simple, healthy and free from avoidable chattering and its consequences. Physically one keeps the body healthy by way of simple food habits, simple exercises and free from excessive stress and strain the body will become flexible and healthy. This will lead one towards healthy, happy and long life. Lastly, materially one will have to constantly avoid accumulation of material objects and keep on unloading them to free from living with clutter of material things and make living simple. This will help to escape from the misery of the mystery of the missing things in day today life either in house or in office.

It was Ralph Waldo Emerson who said that, "Nothing is more simple than greatness; indeed, to be simple is to be great".

This magical pathway may appear simple. But the thorns of difficulty in pursuing this path will disappear if one understands the nature and effectiveness of simplicity and proceed on it to reach its destination of magical life.

> "The price we pay for the complexity of life is too high.
> When you think of all the effort you have to put in—
> telephonic, technological and relational—to alter even the
> slightest bit of behavior in this strange world we call social
> life, you are left pining for the straightforwardness of
> primitive peoples and their physical work"
>
> **Jean Baudrillard**

PATHWAY OF APPRECIATION

Appreciation is noble in thought and in saying loudly too. It is an instantaneous feeling which will arise in everyone's heart unless suppressed by various extraneous thoughts. To appreciate others good word or deed is not only healthy for one's own mind but also for others healthy living. Appreciation spreads a vibration of happiness all round and help to develop feeling of goodness among humans. To appreciate the goodness of nature, good words and deeds of others one will have to necessarily identify the spontaneous feeling and develop it as a habit and continue to nurture for one's own happy living as well as others' happy living with meaning.

This magical pathway although appears clear and straight but many humans ignore it by their self-pride and arrogant way of living. If its importance is realized and this pathway is taken to proceed then it will take everyone to its destination of all round happiness and magical life.

Voltaire wrote that, "Appreciation is a wonderful thing. It makes what is excellent in others belong to us as well."

> "The roots of all goodness lie in the soil of
> appreciation for goodness."
>
> **His Holiness, Dalai Lama**

PATHWAY OF SPIRITUALITY

Humans are essentially spiritual beings. Spirituality, therefore, is a hidden treasure in everyone. To understand and activate spirituality is only to regain one's spiritual nature provided by the creative intelligence–God. Spirituality does not mean renunciation and denouncement of worldly life. Everyone need not be a religious person to practice spirituality in life. Spirituality leads one to a higher level of consciousness. Therefore, one will have to regain the power of spirituality in one's life. For that purpose one will have to take this magical pathway which will lead to a peaceful, stable, healthy, and godly life.

> "The more we engage in spiritual practices,
> the more control we gain over our body, mind and fate."
>
> **Andrew Newberg**

Mark Robert Waldman

Finally, we have to understand that these magical pathways will help one to reach the magical destination of life which are heath, happiness, and wealthy living of a life of fulfillment with meaning. To conclude I would like to quote the following which I found as a gem on my magical pathways which will to some extent summarize what we both have been trying to find out in our one year long dialogue.

> "I believe that imagination is stronger than knowledge—
> myth is more potent than history—dreams are more
> powerful than facts—hope always triumphs over
> experience—laughter is the cure for grief
> —love is stronger than death."
>
> **Robert Fulghum**

"Thank you so much. I really do not know how to thank you for taking me on your magical pathways as a companion for the last twelve months. It is indeed an incredible treasure hunt of magical pathways you have shown me, which I will value, promote, and practice and proceed in all through my life. The journey on the path with you is a rewarding experience. Let there be no end. Let it be a beginning, Thank you again."

"I told you earlier that we need not thank each other. It is a life's journey and the path is laid out for our journey. As you correctly said, let there be no end. Let there always be a beginning. **Goodbye."**

Epilogue

It was a pleasant evening in December. I was sitting under the same tree in Marina Beach, Chennai, where I used to sit and listen to the old and the young when they were having the dialogue over a period of twelve months. After some time, the young one, after finishing his evening walk, came and sat near me. As we both were not able to catch up with our usual morning walk, we went for our evening walk on that day. I told him that I was benefited from the discussions. I have decided to publish them as a book. The young one told me that the discussions have entirely changed his life and it helped him to proceed on the new magical pathways.

For twelve months, they had covered the entire spectrum of human life commencing from the life itself, whether it is mystical, or real and painful or magical, as their first dialogue. The superiority of the nature, the concept of time, the nature and the perception of health, the theory of karma and its perceived impacts on humans, the role the religion and the spirituality plays in humans' life, the true nature and the perception of happiness, the problems of modern life's choices and balance, the effectiveness of yoga and meditation and how the recent scientific researches proved their usefulness even in the present fast and modern days, understanding the purpose and the meaning of life and finally how the magical pathways if one decides to walk will change the life into a magical one were discussed by the old and the young. Although the young one had a different perception of life in the beginning, he slowly embraced the actual truths of life as enunciated by the old one.

After some time, both of us felt the absence of the old one about whom we had been discussing that evening. Suddenly, we felt the vacuum. Also, we realized that many of the usual walkers were missing. We therefore left the beach and proceeded on our way back home. When we were returning, we saw a big funeral procession. Many of the usual walkers were going along with the procession.

We approached one of them to find out what was happening. The gentleman asked us, "How come you people do not know that the old gentleman has passed away in the morning?" At this point of time we both painfully remembered that the old gentleman who used to say 'good day' after the end of every day's discussion had said on the previous day morning 'good bye'. Perhaps he had the premonition of his passing away next day morning. We were naive; not able to connect or understand his last words of taking leave of us from his life's journey.

We found that his body was being taken for cremation. We were shocked, as it was a surprise to us. The old one was on the beach in the previous day in the early morning and had talked to us about the magical pathways. With heavy hearts, we also joined the procession. There were floral tributes for the departed soul all over the roads on his last journey in this world. We went near the coffin to have a last darshan (reverential look) of his face. The body was kept laid in an open coffin with his head raised. The face was so serene and peaceful as we used to see him every day at the beach. We could not bear our grief any longer and said "Goodbye" with heavy hearts and tears in our eyes. Later we slowly moved and joined the mourners.

The silence was eloquent. The sun was slowly setting on the western side of the beach. After a twelve-hour journey from the early hours of the day, the sun was setting in the evening with its yellowish brightness. Although we left the beach and joined the procession, the image of the golden path of the morning sun on the blue sea waters came to our minds. Within twelve hours, the sun had crossed its path and had come to the west from the east to hide itself to rise again with its glorious golden light in the morning of the next day. These sights empowered with their metaphorical message captured us in our extraordinary moments of grief.

When the cremation was over, we were returning home with heavy hearts. The only consolation was that we were carrying the dialogues that the young one had with the old one in our minds.

Also, I had the C.D. wherein I had recorded the dialogues for publication in the form of a book.

The young one was in tears when he remembered the words of the old one when the first conversation started twelve months ago. 'Life never ends. It only changes its course in various phases. No beginning. No end. Life always moves in circles and cycles'. It made me feel very sad. However, we both consoled ourselves that reality will have to be faced and we will have to meet the challenge before us with courage. Also, we felt that his discourses will carry us through in our new magical pathways of our lives. We decided to publish the book in his honor.

The young one made me to remember again the old one's words, which were intuitively told by him on the previous day of his departure. 'It is a life's journey and the path is laid out for our journey. Let there be no end. Let there always be a beginning'.

With our heavy hearts, we took leave of each other with tears in our eyes and with the hope in our hearts that the old one's words will remain eternal.

Brief Details Of
The Author

S.P. CHOCKALINGAM

The author is a post graduate in Economics. He served as a banker.

In 1983, he had an unique privilege of meeting His Holiness Dalai Lama in Jakarta. He shook hands and held H. H. Dalai Lama's hands for quite some time and conversed with him. According to the author this meeting was the greatest transforming and defining moment in his life.

He is practicing yoga and meditation for the last 12 years.

He is a published author of five books in Tamil one of the oldest and classical languages in India. All of them are in poetry form. One is Meenakshi Andhadhi with 100 verses in Anthraksha(Sanskrit)form. This means that the last word in the first verse will become first word of the second verse and it goes on till the 100th verse. This is a unique style of poetry form in Tamil which is called 'Andaadhi'. 'And' means end and 'aadi' means beginning ie. The last word (And) of the first verse becomes the first word ('aadi') of the second verse.

This was made into audio musical C.D. with music set by one of the well known music director and rendered by Sangeetha Kalanidhi Sudha Ragunathan, the famous Carnatic musician in India. This C.D. is sold all over the world wherever Tamil population live. In major temples in India and other temples this C.D. is being played.

He with his wife Mrs. Vijaya lives in Chennai. His children and grand children live in U.S.A.

Bibiliography

Self Matt ers   –   Dr. Phil McGraw

Living as God   –   P Raymond Stewart

Emotional Intelligence   –   Daniel Goleman

SQ-Spiritual Intelligence   –   Danah Zohar and Ian Marshall

The Art of Happiness   –   H H Dalai Lama and
Howard C Cutler

Da Vinci Decoded   –   Michael J Gelb

Atha Nitishatakam   –   Bhartrihari Translated by
Rajendra Tandon

Wisdom of the Heart   –   Alan Cohen

The Present   –   Dr Spencer Johnson

The Alchemist   –   Paulo Coelho

Ping   –   Stuart Avery Gold

Soul to Soul   –   Gary Zukav

Essence of Yoga Vasishtha   –   Translated by Samvid from
Sanskrit

The Biology of Belief   –   Bruce H. Lipton Ph.d

How God Changes Your Brain   –   Andrew Newberg and Mark
Robert Waldman

Freedom from the Known   –   J Krishnamurti

A Celebration of Rumi   –   Andrew Harvey

The Prophet   –   Kahlil Gibran

Reinventing the Body, Resurrecting the Soul	–	Deepak Chopra
Social Intelligence	–	Daniel Goleman
The New Quotable Einstien	–	Edited by Alice Calaprice
Tripurarahasyam	–	Translated from Sanskrit by Samvid
Stillness Speaks	–	Eckhart Tolle.
The Ultimate Happiness	–	Deepak Chopra
Change Your Thoughts Change your life Reflections on Yoga	–	Dr. Wayne. W Dyer
Sutra's of Patanjali	–	T.K.V. Desikachar.
Light on Yoga	–	B.K.S. Iyengar
Love and Survival	–	Dr. Dean Ornish
Same Soul Many Bodies	–	Brian L. Weiss. M.D
The Power of Now	–	Eckhart Tolle
In Search of Mind	–	T.K.V. Desikachar
Understanding Our Mind	–	Thich Nhat Hanh
Reversing Heart Disease	–	Dr. Dean Ornish
The Vision and way of Vasistha	–	Translated from Sanskrit by Samvid
The Shift	–	Dr. Wayne W. Dyer
War of the World Views	–	Deepak Chopra and Leonard Mlodinow
How to Be Happy All the Time	–	Paramahansa Yogananda
An Open Heart	–	H.H.Dalai Lama
Outwitting the Devil	–	Napoleon Hill
Self Power	–	Deepak Chopra
Proof of Heaven	–	Dr. Eben Alexander M.D.

Harmonic Wealth	–	James Arthur Ray
Breaking the Habit of Being Yourself	–	Dr. Joe Dispenza
Zen and the Art of Consciousness	–	Susan Blackmore